A FEW GOOD MEN AND THE ANGRY SEA

A FEW GOOD MEN AND THE ANGRY SEA

Lessons in Disaster Management

Air Commodore Nitin Sathe (Retd)

Published by
Renu Kaul Verma
Vitasta Publishing Pvt Ltd
4348/4C, Ansari Road, Daryaganj
New Delhi - 110 002
info@vitastapublishing.com

ISBN: 978-81-19670-96-3
© Nitin Sathe
First Edition 2025

MRP ₹ 395

All Rights Reserved.
No part of this publication may be reproduced, stored in a retrieval system, or transmitted in any form, or by any means–electronic, mechanical, photocopying, recording or otherwise–without the prior permission of the publisher. Opinions expressed in this book are the authors' own. The publisher is in no way responsible for these.

Layout & Cover Design by Rohit Gautam
Printed at Chaman Enterprises, New Delhi

Contents

Dedication	*vii*
I Salute You	*ix*
Foreword	*xi*

The Dark Brown Sea	1
Christmas and After	15
The First Wave and Then	23
Dotting the Devastation	35
Early Days of Relief	39
Day-to-Day Recovery	45
Rebuilding Brick-by-Brick	65
The Integrated Command	73
Operation Madad	77
Airlifts Continue	83
Disaster on Show	91
The Shock and the Survivors	99

Op Ready	107
Rising like a Phoenix	111
Supreme Commander Comes Calling	115
Rehabilitation	121
The Memorial	127
In Memorium	133
APPENDIX	***143***
IAF Airbase Recovers from the Tsunami	*145*
Carnic, Nature's Wonder	*153*
History of the Airbase	*165*

This one is for you, Daddy

I Salute You

INDIA HAS, for centuries, been vulnerable to a wide range of natural disasters—cyclones, floods, earthquakes, landslides, and tsunamis. These calamities have claimed countless lives, uprooted families, and caused irreparable loss to property and livelihood. The 2004 Indian Ocean tsunami was one of the most devastating such events in recent memory, bringing unprecedented destruction to large parts of coastal India and the Andaman & Nicobar Islands.

This book, first published as a photo-rich coffee table edition, captures my personal journey and that of many others during this catastrophe. I was among the fortunate few who had the honour of serving in the Andaman & Nicobar Islands immediately after the tsunami. What I witnessed—the pain, the resilience, and the unwavering commitment of those who rose to help—changed my life forever.

Disasters of this scale highlight the inescapable necessity of involving the Armed Forces in relief and rehabilitation, especially in developing countries where civil resources may be inadequate. The military's ability to mobilise swiftly, operate in austere conditions, and provide structure in chaos makes it indispensable in such scenarios. Today, India has bolstered its disaster response capability with institutions like the National Disaster Management Authority (NDMA) and the National Disaster Response Force (NDRF), which are now better trained and equipped to face emergencies. Yet, the synergy between civil agencies and the Armed Forces remains vital.

This revised edition, made more affordable and accessible with black-and-white photographs, is my humble effort to share not just stories of courage and coordination, but also to underline the urgent need for disaster awareness and preparedness across all sections of society. May these stories inspire a deeper understanding of disasters—not just as events of destruction, but as calls to unite, respond, and rebuild.

— Air Commodore Nitin Sathe (Retd)
May 2025

एयर चीफ मार्शल अरूप राहा
प वि से में अ वि से में वा मे ए डी सी
Air Chief Marshal Arup Raha
PVSM AVSM VM ADC

Tel : (011) Off : 23012517
Res : 23017300
Fax : 23018453
Email : hawkeye@bol.net.in

वायु सेना मुख्यालय
नई दिल्ली-110106
Air Headquarters
New Delhi - 110 106

Foreword

I FEEL privileged to write the foreword to this first-hand account of the role played by the Armed Forces in general and our Air Force in particular, in the aftermath of the tsunami of 26 December 2004.

The Indian Air Force has always been at the forefront of Humanitarian Assistance and Disaster Relief (HADR) operations within and outside the borders of our great nation. Crew from the helicopter and transport fleet have proven their courage in many a mission to provide assistance and support to those in distress, and have been instrumental in saving many lives in difficult situations.

The Tsunami Relief Operation in 2004 was one of the major HADR missions undertaken by our Armed Forces, besides the ones in the wake of the Bhuj earthquake and, more recently, in Uttarakhand and Srinagar. This book is a tribute to the valiant efforts of men and women in uniform who, with total disregard to their personal safety and well-being, take on such tasks and complete them with a smile on their faces.

The tsunami of 26 December 2004 was preceded by a high intensity earthquake whose epicentre lay below the sea near Banda Aceh in Indonesia. What followed was an intense wave generated over the ocean floor that travelled in all directions to several continents. At landfall, a massive tsunami was generated that devastated everything and everyone in its path. The island of Car Nicobar was one of the worst-hit regions in our country. The bustling Air Force Station at Car Nicobar was all but razed to the ground. Our Air Force was quick to react and a team of dedicated air-warriors was immediately dispatched to the island to take charge of the station and help in the relief and rehabilitation efforts. The author—a Wing Commander then, volunteered for the job and was duly entrusted with the responsibility to supervise the operations at the base along with coordination of rescue and relief efforts as the Task Force Commander. This book is a personal account of his experiences in disaster management, as well as the role played by all sections of society, the Government and the Armed Forces, who formed a formidable team to bring back normalcy to the islands in record time.

It has been ten years since the disaster and the islands have recovered to a large extent. Besides giving an insight into the events as they unfolded, this book will also serve as a repertoire of facts, figures and anecdotes as we move on to newer and bigger challenges.

I am sure more of our gallant men and women engaged in such demanding operations will be inspired by this book to wield a pen for the benefit of future generations.

December 2014
Jai Hind!

Air Chief Marshal
Chief of the Air Staff

Aerial view of the destruction caused by the 2004 tsunami

The Dark Brown Sea

HOT AND foetid air filled the aircraft the moment the doors were opened. The salty smell of the sea, mixed with the trenchant odour of rotting flora and fauna, filled our nostrils.

As the aircraft approached the island, all of us assigned to this mission craned our necks to get a first look at the devastation through the small round windows.

We saw a dark brown sea with huge trunks of trees and debris floating on it. Large tracts of forest had been flattened as if someone had sliced through them with a knife.

The runway was brown, like the sea, full of rubble, sand and broken tree trunks on the eastern side.

Just enough of the runway had been cleared of this detritus to allow us to make a safe landing.

As we taxied into the parking slot all we could see was rubbish strewn all around as if someone searching for something had rummaged through the whole island and left the debris spread all over.

Six Days Before

Six days earlier, on 26 December 2004, on a cold afternoon in Patiala, Punjab, where I was posted as Commander of a small Indian Air Force base, I was getting ready for a post-Christmas barbeque, when my nine-year old daughter Aishwarya came running up to me and asked, 'Baba, do you know what a tsunami is?'

She had picked up the word—then only vaguely known to most of us—from watching a television news bulletin.

As I watched the news that evening, I learnt of the devastating impact of that natural phenomenon on the eastern and southern seaboard of India.

The Indian Air Force Station, located on the island of Car Nicobar in the Andaman & Nicobar Islands in the Bay of Bengal, had been completely destroyed, I learnt. Friends of mine were posted at the Car Nicobar base and I was very concerned about their safety. Over a hundred IAF personnel and their families were feared dead.

The next day brought grimmer tidings. The tsunami had killed thousands of people and devastated property all over the southern peninsular region of the Indian sub-continent and elsewhere in South Asia.

I called colleagues and seniors in Delhi to find out what was happening. They told me of plans to assign a

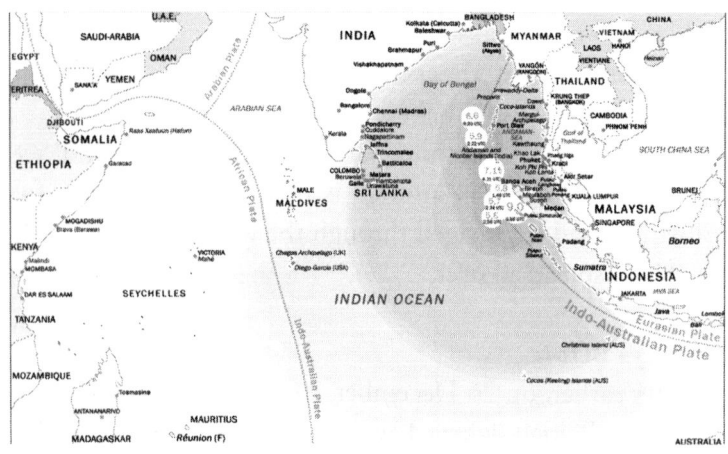

Rescue, Relief and Rehabilitation team of officers and men to Car Nicobar. Those three words—rescue, relief and rehabilitation (RRR)—were going to be part of my daily vocabulary for the next year.

I volunteered to be part of the team. Some of my seniors shooed me away, advising me to enjoy my command instead. I have always been the gung-ho sort, so rather than be deterred by such advice, my resolve to be part of the Car Nicobar mission only got stronger.

The more I thought about it, the more I was convinced that I was cut out for the job. It seemed that Air Headquarters thought so too, for I soon received orders to join the mission.

I was thrilled that someone there felt that I was the man for the job! Later, I learnt that my name had been suggested by one of my earlier Commanders, now posted at the operations branch at Air HQ.

On a New Year, the Journey Begins

I was given just twenty-four hours to pack my bags and travel to Delhi to get my orders. The buzz was that the rescue operation would last about three months.

The new team reaches Car Nicobar

The next day went by in a flurry of activity. A haircut down to the scalp, toiletries to last a while, sufficient clothes and medicines for everyday problems were packed. My better half insisted I take along some snacks in case there was nothing to eat for the first few days.

Lists were made, analysed and remade. I didn't want my

'household' to be too heavy to manage. I was bubbling with excitement, but I detected tension in my family.

My wife fretted and fumed at the thought of staying separated for a long time. She was also worried about my safety but was confident that I would be able to take on this journey into the unknown without much of a problem. To be honest, deep down I felt some anxiety too, tinged with fear. After some tearful moments with my family, I flew to Delhi on 31 December 2004. New Year's Eve was spent walking around the Officers' Mess at the Palam airbase. The New Year's Eve had been cancelled due to the catastrophe.

The news on television did nothing to dispel our apprehensions. There had been more tremors and fears of more tsunamis.

Take-off for Chennai was at six o'clock the next morning. We had to report two hours earlier for a host of formalities to be carried out prior to our departure. For those of us on this assignment, the year 2005 arrived while we were asleep. I spent a somewhat uncomfortable and anxious night tossing and turning, wondering what the morrow was to bring.

The departure lounge at Palam next morning was a flurry of activity. Two An-32 aircraft were being loaded with our paraphernalia and the Vice Chief of Air Staff was due to arrive at 5.45 am.

Villagers walking to higher ground (left); Rushing towards the relief helicopter (right)

There were injections to be taken to avoid becoming victims of typhoid, cholera, yellow fever and other diseases that invariably follow such a calamity. Mefloquine and Doxycycline tablets were doled out to protect us from malaria. Nearly ten years later, I can still remember the horrible after-taste!

The local administration had put up a series of desks at the airport for each activity and the long line of airmen went from desk to desk getting their jabs and tablets and completing the necessary paperwork before heading out to the aircraft with their luggage. We were also handed over some emergency equipment like life boats, communication sets, tents, first aid boxes and emergency rations to last us for the initial few days.

The Vice Chief briefed us about the gravity of the situation and what was expected of us. The seventy-strong rescue and rehabilitation team would be led by Group Captain Ravi Dhar. It consisted of eleven officers from various branches of the Air Force and airmen from different departments and sections.

As a helicopter pilot, I was to be the Chief Operations Officer (COO) of the base, in charge of all flying operations.

I was also to be the 'Task Force Commander', a job that was a little different and more demanding. This work entailed planning, coordinating, organising and executing all the rescue, relief and rehabilitation efforts undertaken from the base to the various islands.

Besides this, I had to ensure that all operations-related infrastructure and equipment was kept in working condition all the time. This included operating surfaces, safety services, air traffic services, rescue services, meteorology, communications, computers and a host of other operations-related issues which ensured that we had a safe and conducive operational environment at base.

Additional helicopters were being flown in from the IAF base in Gorakhpur in the state of Uttar Pradesh to augment the available fleet in Car Nicobar. The only way these could be ferried in was through Myanmar and therefore would take a couple of days to arrive; until then, we would use the three helicopters available at Car Nicobar.

We had a foretaste of the disaster on our arrival at Tambaram Air Force base in Chennai, where we stopped for a night's rest after a hopping flight through Hyderabad. Here we were joined by more members of our team, including the Contingent Commander, Group Captain Ravi Dhar. Most of the surviving families, who had been on Car Nicobar when the tsunami struck, had been flown to Tambaram along with some local civilians in one IL-76 and two An-32 aircraft on 27 December. They were clearly in a state of shock. Some of them had lost family and were inconsolable. It was a heart-wrenching sight.

The civilian population evacuated from the island was handed over to the civilian administration in Chennai. It was said that their actual struggle began after reaching Chennai. These civilians had no family in Chennai and nowhere to go. Most of them found their way back to the islands as soon as communication improved.

The situation was different for the Air Force families. A massive reception centre had been set up for them at Tambaram and as the families arrived, they were seen by a team of doctors, first aid administered and those needing further treatment rushed to the nearest military hospital. The others were taken care of by families in the station as house guests.

I met up with a friend from the Merchant Navy in Chennai. He was on a mission to help villages near Nagapattinam, which had been devastated by the tsunami. He told me what he had seen during the week along the Tamil Nadu coast. It was indeed a sad picture.

It would be a similar situation at Car Nicobar, I thought. The only difference would be that local help would be unavailable on those islands, so far away from the Indian mainland, where almost everyone would have been affected. That's why we were going there anyway, I reflected. We had our job cut out for us.

I indulged in treating myself to some good sumptuous food that evening, knowing fairly well that we won't be getting much for the initial few days on arrival.

Taking Charge of the Eerie Silence
We took off from Chennai at four o' clock in the morning on 2 January 2005 on the last leg of our journey to the tsunami struck islands.

Car Nicobar's Station Commander, Group Captain V V 'Bandy' Bandopadhyay and his Chief Operations Officer, Wing Commander P 'Churpi' Maheshwar, received us at Car Nicobar's devastated airbase when we landed.

Both men had battled the sudden catastrophe and its aftermath for the last six days and had spent sleepless nights. But they both looked to be in fine shape and were upbeat—a characteristic of officers and men of the Armed Forces.

The officers and men who were leaving had to quickly hand over whatever had survived; brief us, and leave by the same aircraft that got us in.

Bandy and Churpi stayed on for the next two days to update us on some of the significant aspects of administration, maintenance and operations at this far-flung base.

Chief Operations Officer Wg Cdr P Maheshwar in his makeshift office

Airlift for the first of the survivors by IL-76

All personnel who had lost their near and dear ones were evacuated from the island along with surviving family members, barring the few who were desperately searching for those still missing.

As the aircraft took off for its return journey to the mainland, an eerie silence descended, broken only by the whining of the wind. We were on our own now, marooned in the midst of destruction. Our mission was about to begin.

What is a Tsunami?

The word 'tsunami' is said to be of Japanese origin and means 'harbour wave'. These are high frequency low amplitude waves generated by seismic activity on the ocean floor, vertically displacing the overlying water in the ocean.

These waves travel at a speed of up to 700-800 kilometre per hour above the ocean floor. As they reach the shallow waters of the continental shelf, they transform into waves of larger amplitude and low frequency and travel at speeds up to 70 kmph. The huge mass of water at this speed can smash through literally anything in its path once it hits land.

The waves are typically 10 to 15 metres high (and can go as high as 25 to 30 metres) and can cause colossal destruction up to about one to three kilometre inland. More often than not, these waves, formed under the ocean due to smaller earthquakes, die out and don't manifest themselves as destructive tsunamis. Any earthquake of above 7.5 on the Richter scale is likely to cause a large tsunami wave of destructive nature if many other conditions are met. A large percentage of these would still peter out by themselves.

The 26 December 2004 tsunami had been preceded by an earthquake of 9.0 on the Richter scale, with its epicentre near the city of Banda Aceh on the Indonesian island of Sumatra, in the early hours of 0628 hours IST.

This was the second severest earthquake ever recorded in history. The earthquake's epicentre was 10 kilometre below the surface of the ocean, along two tectonic plates. The fault created along the tectonic plates was about a 1,000 kilometre in length, aligned in a north-south direction. This generated a wave travelling in an east-west direction, which had enough energy to travel for about 4,500 km, to hit some parts of the eastern shores of Africa 24 hours later.

The first recorded tsunami in India dates back to 31

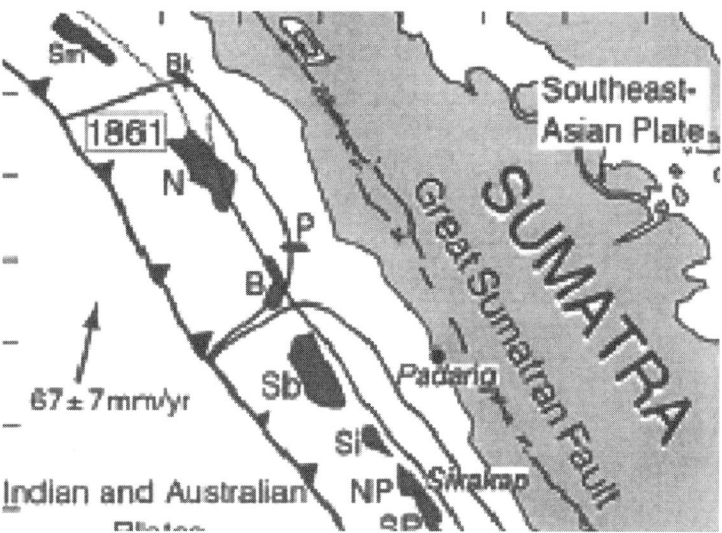

December 1881. An earthquake of magnitude 7.5 on the Richter scale, with its epicentre believed to have been above the sea just off the shoreline of Car Nicobar Island, caused a small tsunami.

Power of the Earthquake
The total energy released by the 2004 earthquake has been estimated as 3.35 Exajoules (3.35 x 10^{18} Joules), as noted by the Royal Geographic Society. This is equivalent to 930 terawatt hours of electric power—as much as the entire United States consumes in eleven days!

The earthquake can be compared to a 0.8 Gigaton TNT explosion which can cause shock waves across the planet. The entire earth's surface is estimated to have moved vertically by up to a centimetre. This shift of mass and massive release of energy slightly altered the earth's rotation and also caused a 'wobble' on its axis, reported various science journals and media articles.

Surveys of the ocean floors have suggested that the 2004 earthquake caused extensive changes in the topography of the ocean floor. The faults that were created led to massive landslides several kilometre long. The force of the water thus displaced caused huge lateral movement of the solid ocean floor, which is believed to have been dragged as much as 10 kilometre. Such was the gigantic nature of this earthquake.

Before this one, the last recorded tsunami in India occurred on 26 June 1941, caused by an earthquake that exceeded 8.5 on the Richter scale. It caused extensive damage to the Andaman Islands. There are no other well-documented records of tsunamis in India although during my interactions with the local population on the island, I was told that folklore has it that a tsunami had occurred on Car Nicobar Island about 99 years ago.

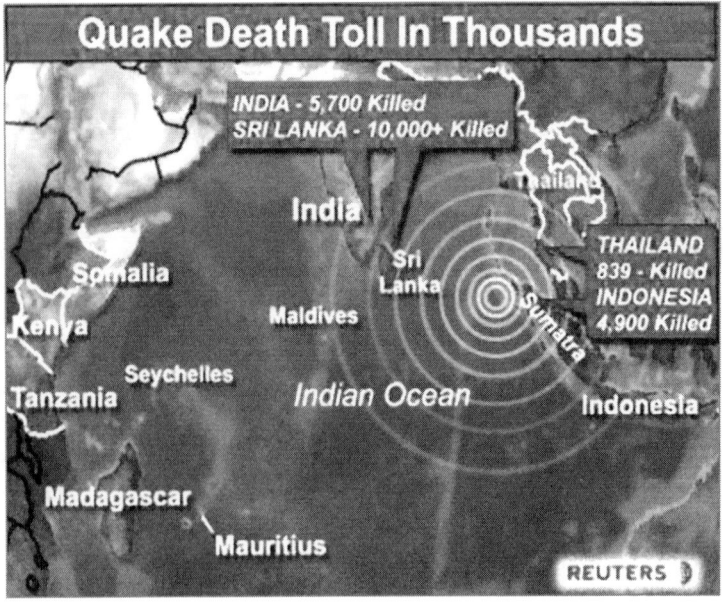

Death toll of the 2004 tsunami

The Dark Brown Sea | 13

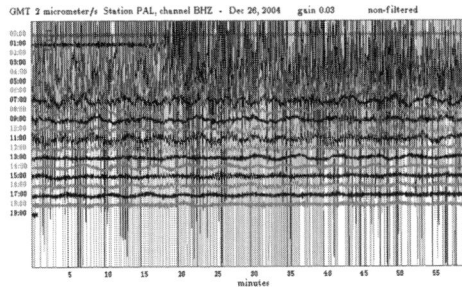

Records from US Geological Survey: Location and magnitude (as recorded by the Lamont Doherty Seismographs at Columbia University) provided the sequence of earthquakes, with some of them being above 6.0 in the Richter Scale.

Open source image from www.flickr.com

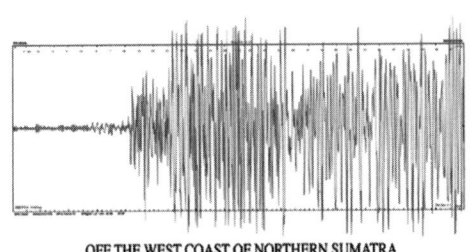

Open source image from http://www2.ohiodnr.com

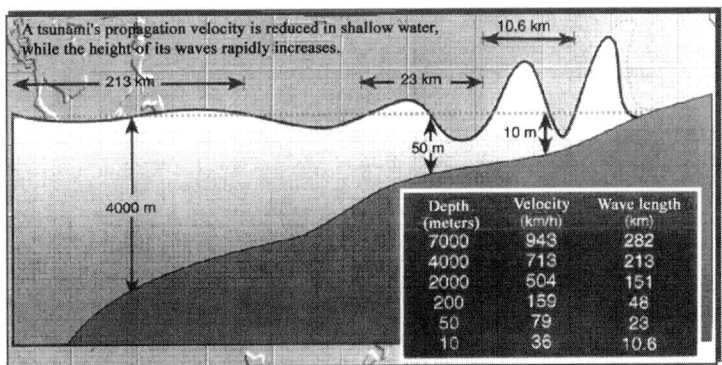

Open source image from http://www.senat.fr

The December 2004 tsunami resulted in the death of 10,136 people on India's East Coast, but there is no knowing how many more were unaccounted for.
Source: Govt of India

Car Nicobar

The Island of Car Nicobar is about 1,500 kilometre east of Chennai and almost the same distance south of Kolkata. It takes four-and-a-half hours to arrive on the island from Chennai by a slow moving propeller aircraft like the *Antonov-32*. The sea route is an experience in itself and takes about forty-eight hours.

Christmas and After

SQUADRON LEADER Selson Rodrigues hosted a Christmas party at his home near the beach that year. Almost all the officers and their families stationed at the Indian Air Force base on the island attended the celebrations which continued well into the night.

Plans were made for a beach dance party on New Year's Eve. The bachelors wanted the party to be held in the anteroom at the Officers' Mess, which had recently been fitted with disco lights and a huge music system. These young officers felt that the station had had too many parties by the sea and 2005 should be brought in differently.

The party at the Rodrigues' home wound up well past midnight. A couple of hours later (0628 hours IST), strong tremors shook the island. The residents were jolted out of their sleep by the cracking noise that accompanied the tremors. This lasted for almost six to eight minutes, making walls fracture and fixtures fall all over. More aftershocks followed in a few minutes. It seemed that the entire island was in a continuous swaying motion.

The islands are prone to high seismic activity, so those stationed on Car Nicobar were familiar with earthquakes. This one, though, was gigantic compared to the ones they had experienced so far. Flying Officer DJ Bhandarkar, a still serving officer who is one of the survivors of the 2004 tsunami, describes it graphically in his diary:

Flying Officer DJ Bhandarkar

In my sleep, I felt as if someone was shaking me very vigorously. I opened my eyes. The bed on which I was sleeping got pushed away and crashed against the cupboard which was almost two feet away and came back. I was shocked. The fan above was shaking from side to side so violently that all the blades had bent. All around there was a haunting sound coming from the ground. The walls were shaking like paper, the floor was shaking, moving up and down with a very severe screeching sound coming from the walls of the house. I saw water seeping in from the overgrowth with tremendous force and it was heading in our direction.

Telephones rang and discussions took place. The officers started trooping out of their homes and stood talking to each other across the fences, unaware at the time of what was in store for them.

Even as they were discussing the situation, some of the officers noticed the Station Commander, Group Captain VV Bandopadhyay, whizzing by in his car. Bandy wanted to find out what damage had been caused to the hangars, service property and the airmen's accommodation. He was most worried about the hangars since they had been declared weak and fragile by experts who had examined them recently.

As the bewildered personnel stood looking out towards the sea, they were stunned to discover that the water had withdrawn much more than it did even during very low tides. As a result, the brilliant coral, glistening in multiple colours, was exposed from under the water for the first time.

Intrigued, some adventurous officers grabbed their cameras and rushed to the shoreline.

The sea continued to recede and the officers had an eyeful of the brilliant blues, reds, oranges and yellows of the exposed corals, little understanding the sinister implications of this beautiful sight.

Squadron Leader NS Dihot had just bought a video camera and decided this was an opportunity not to be missed. He dashed down to the beach to get the footage he wanted.

A damaged camera was washed ashore a few days later; the man was lost forever.

After a while, the sea appeared to return to normal, except for the strong waves and constant churning.

The water level now started to rise and soon crossed the high-tide mark. It was as if the ocean was issuing a warning of what was in store.

Had the IAF personnel been aware of the signs that indicated an impending tsunami wave, I believe the casualties would have been fewer. But in the panic induced by the tremors, the instinct was to stay close to their homes, which were situated near the beach.

The water continued to rise to the plinth level of the houses, and then inundated the ground floors closest to the sea.

That got people moving. Since the runway was on much higher ground, they began moving towards it. But some still sought refuge on the first floor of their homes or those of their friends; the women were reluctant to venture out in their nightclothes.

One panic-stricken group of about twenty-five people decided to climb above the first floor where there was just enough place for the overhead water tanks. Later, this decision was to prove fatal.

Many people had run to the relatively higher ground of the runway of the Air Force Station which began filling up with people, some of whom had managed to pack a few of their belongings. The security wall on the far side of the runway was ordered to be broken down so that should the waters reach this far, the people could run towards higher ground beyond.

Soon after the earthquake, the sea retreated, exposing the magnificent colourful coral

Labourers housed in a camp close to the sea had been the most resourceful. They had quickly moved themselves and their bags to higher ground on the edge of the runway. They had been brought in from the mainland by contractors engaged in construction activity on the airbase. Most of them were from Bihar and Odisha and had some idea of how to cope with flood situations that occurred frequently in their home towns.

Group Captain Bandopadhyay drove up and down the main road, giving lifts to people moving towards the runway. Subsequently, his car was washed away by the first wave and he was reported missing. He miraculously escaped and returned to camp after a few hours.

Junior Warrant Officer Sreesa Kumar was a young Non Commissioned Officer posted at Carnic base. He still serves in the IAF and describes very vividly the events of that fateful day:

Junior Warrant Officer Sreesa Kumar

It was morning and I was sleeping in my ground floor quarter with my family consisting of two children aged seven and three. The ground shook violently and I fell off my bed. Realising that it was an earthquake, my first reaction was to push my wife and children under the bed to avoid any injury. I had to crawl on my fours to get to the door which was jammed shut. I panicked and went towards the rear door which was luckily kept open for the fresh breeze with the wire mesh door bolted. I broke open the wire mesh and escaped out of the house with my family. While we sat down outside getting our bearings, we saw the Station Commander driving by, stopping and asking everybody about their well being.

We heard people say that the sea had receded and then saw

that some people were running away shouting *bhago bhago (run, run)*. We started running towards the radar ramp which was close to the sea. Half way I realised that the ramp was full of people and decided to run back to get my scooter which had fallen on its side. While driving along the road towards the guard room, water came up to the footrest of the scooter and luckily, my scooter didn't stall. I noticed an MES JCO following me with his family of four just a few yards behind. As I looked back, I saw him being washed away along with his two children. Later on, we came to know that he had lost his wife and daughter and managed to save his son from the sea. I also saw the Station Commander's car turning turtle right in front of my eyes—the Station Commander was just getting into it.

Having dropped his family to a seemingly safe place, Sreesa went back on his scooter to check on the MES JCO. En route, he saw his friend and colleague Sergeant Joy, whose

Waiting for rescue, people gather on the edge of the runway

An upturned vessel at the dock in Port Blair

family was tired of running and sitting on the roadside. He helped the lady and the child to safety; he asked Joy to continue running behind his scooter.

As the survivors got their wits about them, the first thing was to look for their loved ones and friends. All the bodies that were found were taken near the tarmac and covered with whatever material was available. Some inconsolable airmen were seen carrying their dead children on their shoulders the whole day. Some of them wanted to go all over the station shouting themselves hoarse, trying to find the lost members of their family.

Later, as we began the rehabilitation process, we did get a number of survivors back to the island as astrologers they met had told them that their family was alive. Some went to the extent of giving a large number of advertisements in local dailies of their missing family members.

Debris at the shore after the tsunami

The First Wave and Then

THE FIRST giant wave hit the island from the south, approximately forty-five minutes after the earthquake. Survivors described it as a huge wall of brown water, about thirty to forty-five feet high and a kilometre-and-a-half wide, travelling at breakneck speed. It travelled inland, taking with it all that it encountered.

Behind it, a short while later, came another large wave from the south-east, which tore apart whatever was still left standing.

Wing Commander BS Krishna Kumar was the Commanding Officer of the helicopter unit at Car Nicobar. In his recollection of that terrible day, he narrates how, once the violent earthquake had subsided, he thought the worst was over:

Wing Commander
BS Krishna Kumar

I entered my bedroom and was taking off the top of my night suit when I heard a loud cry, presumably from my wife—'*Bhago!*' or maybe it was 'Run!' I paused. There is no earthquake. So what is it? Something deep down told me there was something amiss and the NDA (National Defence Academy)-inculcated survival instinct told me—just run.

I did not even wait to wear my top or waste time collecting my specs and slippers. I just ran out. I saw my wife struggling to open the gate. My unit officer, Vijay, shouted, 'Sir, run, the sea is coming in'.

He had seen the water retreating and then the surge of the sea. I looked back and saw the sea had entered our lawns. It was churned up water, like an invasion of the mighty ocean. Perplexed, I told my wife and children to run. We were all guided by Flt Lt Vijay towards the runway—his situational awareness was great, I can say in retrospect. The runway was a kilometre-and-a-half inland and a few feet above sea level. Was the island sinking? We did not know.

Events developed faster than memory can record. I saw my wife giving up, I told her 'Don't!' Later, she told me that she had looked back and had seen a huge wave hitting our house, then the second one, over the house, right behind us. She thought it was all over. Wg Cdr Shukla came in a car and picked up my wife and son. I and my daughter continued to run. I peeled off at the last turn to the runway, telling my daughter to continue running towards the runway. I diverted to the motor transport section, picked up my official car and drove back, blissfully unaware of what was happening. I was sure that many families would be struggling to run with their children. We were still in our night clothes and barefoot. I picked up many people. I could see death in their eyes. As I dropped them off and was returning for a second round, the Station Commander crossed me. He said, 'Krishna, just get airborne and see what is happening'.

I turned back. On the dispersal, helicopters were shaken by the earthquake, and the dispersal had cracked. There was no time to waste. The crew was available as we always had a helicopter and crew ready for ASSR (Air Sea Search and Rescue). I borrowed a pair of slippers, wore my Mae

West and along with Vijay, Flight Engineer Das and Gunner Sharma, got airborne in the Mi-8 in a minute or so. The start up was so fast that in retrospect I can't believe that an Mi-8 can be started up and airborne in such a short time. That human performance matches the demand placed on one was proven by this quick reaction which, of course, was a pure team effort.

A devastated building after the tsunami

Aerial views of the devastation that the tsunami left in its wake

As Krishna took off, he had a bird's eye view of what had happened and the continuing devastation. Circling over the island, he contacted Port Blair on high frequency radio and passed on the first information report to the headquarters of the Andaman and Nicobar Command who were desperate to know what was happening at this forward base. 'What we saw was unbelievable and shocking,' Krishna writes in his recollections. He adds:

'Waves, giant ones, were lashing the entire domestic area. We did an orbit to assess what was happening, transmitted to SATCO (Senior Air Traffic Controller) Sqn Ldr Satyender, who by now had salvaged a VHF communication set from the damaged Air Traffic Control Tower. 'Satyen, the domestic area is washed off, the runway side seems to be safe, but break the boundary wall and ask the folks to be ready to run further inwards if required', I told him.

We decided to press on with the rescue operations. We saw a few people waving at us from roof tops, but as we were positioning to pick them up, they went missing. The buildings collapsed like a deck of cards. Trees were uprooted and huge trees were floating to and fro like tiny branches. The sea was violent and the water level had gone over the buildings' top floor. Anything could happen, I thought. We started winching up people from roof tops.

The Air Traffic Control tower roof had collapsed and had sandwiched all the equipment inside. This meant there was no immediate means of communication with the mainland or Port Blair, barring the equipment on the helicopter, which had a limited range.

Krishna spotted Bandy's car wedged between some trees outside the station premises. But there was no sign of the Station Commander.

The Immediate Rescue

As Krishna continued to fly all over the base, he saw a large group of people on the radar ramp, waving out to him. Both ends of the ramp, which housed the radar antenna, had been broken by the fury of the tsunami wave and the 250 people who had taken refuge there were stranded on top. Krishna decided to rescue them and deposit them on the runway.

The ramp had been shaken up, was tilted, and obviously weakened. Krishna hovered as low as he possibly could over the crowd, and rescued the marooned people.

Infrastructure tilted and broken by the force of the sea

Krishna Kumar Describes this Rescue

We saw a large crowd of around 250 people who had taken refuge on the Radar Unit ramp. The ramp had already got separated from the two ends and another onslaught of waves would have taken away those lives. There was no time to lose. Winching of these people started—they were a mix of gents and ladies of all ages. Everyone was so panic-stricken that there was no control and people were hanging on to the winch cable in groups. Sgt B Singh of our unit, who was amongst them, managed to control the crowd and we winched up people, sometimes two at a time.

One more helicopter was pressed into service on the orders of Krishna Kumar.

DJ and Devinder asked for my permission to start up the second helicopter. Considering their experience level, I asked them to start and wait for two of my experienced pilots, Sqn Ldr Sachin Kadam and Nijjar. But, neither turned up. Sachin had been washed away and Nijjar was badly injured, having been caught in the waves and losing both his children.

The water had swept the dispersal while they were starting up, bringing in hordes of branches and trees. A huge cement-mixing unit was thrown over by a giant wave which missed the starting helicopter by a few feet. The ground crew was washed away, but was rescued, so they aborted the start, and later resumed when the water subsided a little.

The broken radar ramp from where about 250 people were rescued

Surveying the wreck

The Chief Operations Officer, Wg Cdr Maheshwar, surprised me by joining the team. Later, I learnt that he along with his family had a miraculous escape, having been in the waves for a couple of minutes. The rescue operations continued with the second helicopter joining in.

Krishna Kumar adds
We pulled out people from rooftops and balconies. Then, the waves seemed to subside. I transmitted the same to ground control, but asked people to be ready in case of another wave.

The rescue had to be accelerated. There was a bit of place on the road that was beginning to clear up. We landed the Mi-8 in that less than 7m x 7m space and picked up people. I had switched over to the second helicopter, as the fuel in the first was over.

Flying on an empty stomach without specs for more than five hours gave me a headache. On the ground, the rescue was being coordinated by the Chief Operations Officer and team. I got back and, unable to hold myself up, lay down on the runway's shoulder. I felt my chest was about to burst. But then I realised I was the lucky one; at least for the time being all my family was safe.

My fellow men had lost their near and dear ones, some husbands, some wives, some wife and children, some children, some had to be totally written off. The whole AF Station had gathered around the runway. There was not even drinking water left. The Station Health Care Centre was completely washed away, and so was Dr Garima Sharma. A Dornier from Port Blair had landed by then on the broken runway, along with Air Cmde Vijay Kumar.

The District Commissioner and Superintendent of Police then requested us for an aerial survey of the island. I wasn't aware of the damage to other parts of the island, as my assessment was that the waves had hit the island from the east and so only the Air Force side was affected. We got airborne and discovered that the water had entered the entire island from all sides, wiping out villages up to three kilometre inland.

Sqn Ldr Sudhakar and Flt Lts Devender, Sreenivas and Pramod Nair did a great job by retrieving the bodies, an operation that continued for three days, till the CISF team arrived. They would set out sniffing for decomposed bodies, identify them with whatever was available, and burn them with aviation fuel (contaminated with sea water).

Rescue continues

We lost 116 people from the Air Force; the brunt was borne by the officers as the officers' quarters were in the line of fire, ie. close to the scenic sea. The island lost nearly 3,000 people.

My house was completely washed away, my car was crushed under a tree, I felt the futility of material possessions and felt a deep sense of empathy for the ones who lost their kith and kin.

Once the waters had receded, and the initial brunt of the devastation and rescue effort internalised, almost the entire station gathered near the ATC building to take stock of the situation.

'The wail of the grieved ones was strong enough to rip apart the strongest of hearts while the joy of people reuniting with their families was also beyond imagination', wrote a survivor in his diary. 'The ones who wept did not do so for their homes or belongings; and the ones who rejoiced did so in spite of it.'

'Walls make houses and hearts make homes'—a well known proverb was well understood by all at that point of time.

Another daring rescue undertaken by Krishna Kumar was of an MES technician working atop a water truck when the wave struck. The vehicle was thrown towards the water tank and this gentleman managed to hang on to the metal ladder leading to the top of the tank. As the water receded, the man found himself unable to either go up or come down the ladder in sheer fright.

KK saw him hanging on for dear life and winched him to safety on to his helicopter.

The first panic subsided and a roundup of all men was ordered to take stock of how many had survived. The whole station was practically on the tarmac in front of the ATC building. In the late afternoon, the first Dornier-228 (a small

MES-IB destroyed

The brave young men of the helicopter unit who were part of the initial rescue

aircraft) arrived from Port Blair with some relief. This was followed by an An-32 later in the evening.

The aeroplanes carried some cooked rice and pickle along with some loaves of bread and jam. Some fruit was found in the ration store and all this was promptly distributed amongst the children and ladies. Some enterprising airmen climbed the coconut trees to pluck coconuts for water. As they sat eating in the wee hours of the evening, the earth shook again several times. The ladies now started singing *bhajans* (hymns) to pacify themselves. All were at their wits end.

In the next two days, Sreesa and his friends went scouring the island and the base for survivors. It was dangerous to wade through water and debris but there was no choice. In all, 25 bodies were recovered and given a mass burial later. Sreesa, during one such search, came across his own uniform floating in the water. He recovered his name tab and rank badges and promptly wore them on his overalls which he had managed from the logistics section. As he checked his front pocket, he found Rs 5,000 which he had been paid the previous day as salary. He offered this money to survivors leaving the island in the IL-76 the next day.

Over the next few years the survivors were made to undergo extensive counselling so that they could lead normal lives once again. Sreesa's family has completely recovered as have many more. They do keep in touch and have formed a survivors group on social media.

Station Medicare Centre in ruins, only the porch survived

Dotting the Devastation

WE SAW the horrific devastation caused by the tsunami ourselves in time. It was of Biblical proportions, as if we were creatures on Noah's Arc watching our worlds float by. Someone's clothes, someone's car....

Before the RRR teams arrived in Carnic, the first lot of bodies had been given a mass burial. A total of twenty-five bodies were found and these were buried in a large rectangular grave dug right next to the runway. But in the days to come, we saw many more victims of the killer waves scattered across the island.

We saw cars, bikes and trucks smashed and piled on top of each other. Gas cylinders punctuated the chaotic scene. The station canteen and the Medicare Centre right next to it were buried under sand. The VVIP lodge on the beach was completely destroyed and what remained of the Station Commander's house was just the hard plinth.

A fridge was hanging on a tree a good 30-35 feet from the ground—it became one of those sights that post-tsunami visitors were taken to see. We saw the first floor of one house separated from the ground floor and flung about a hundred metres away—a force we could not believe that water could generate.

Hindu deities found intact after the deadly tsunami

Later, we discovered that rounded buildings like lighthouses were not damaged since the shape did not offer resistance to the flow of water. Most of the temples and churches along the shoreline were intact, as if their presiding deities had shown some mercy on themselves!

A few days later, we found in the floating debris a small wooden cubicle with idols of Hindu gods intact. We were told that it had travelled across the ocean from Indonesia. The local administration promptly installed the cubicle near their office, and it became another article of interest to visitors.

The island's only arterial road was washed off at various places, cutting off villages from each other. The main gate at the Air Force Station was completely cut off from the rest of the base. We were able to cut our way to this gate, only a week after our arrival on the island.

All houses in the villages along the sea were completely destroyed. Human loss was estimated at between 3,000 to 3,500 lives, almost 18 per cent of Car Nicobar's population. Besides the locals and the IAF personnel, the island had a large population of transient labour, some of whom also perished.

We saw huge diesel containers of the Indian Oil Corporation, each of 80,000 litre capacity, lying broken, torn from their mountings and resting on their sides. One of these also blocked the entry to the station.

Most of the fuel in the containers had been washed away, and the local residents managed to siphon off whatever was left. The containers had to be cut and rolled out of the way to make way for traffic.

Road leading to the accommodation

Fuel containers displaced by the tsunami

The mighty IL-76

Early Days of Relief

THE DISTRICT headquarters at Car Nicobar was almost intact, barring a few cracks to some buildings. The administrative offices here were established on high ground, away from the sea shore. The British, who had built them, had an understanding of nature and topography and had planned for it, situating their headquarters in the safest possible place.

The first rehabilitation centre was established here in a school playing field about three days after the disaster. There was no loss of life amongst the district officials reported by the administration. However, the officials seemed to be completely overwhelmed by the enormity of the disaster. While they tried to do whatever they could, it was left to the Defence Services to bring some semblance of order, and plan and execute the relief operations.

Over the next few days, the island gave the impression of a ghost town. Local people came out to salvage whatever they could from the debris and from the shops that were buried under the sand.

There were also incidences of locals entering the broken and abandoned homes inside the Air Force Station, foraging for whatever they could find for their immediate survival. We could do little to stop this for the first few days; our first task was to get the runway operational.

Later, we were able to tackle this problem. For the families of the station personnel, immediate relief was available from the logistics section which stored adequate stocks of clothing and dry rations, but the local population had no access to anything similar, except for some minimal rations the district administration had in stock. We helped all those villagers who came to request us for rations and material help in the first few days.

Some of the islands in the archipelago such as Chowra and Trinket had been cut into half by the waters. What had been good solid earth just a few days ago was now water and marshy land rendered useless forever by the sea.

The IAF base lost about 160 acres of good land due to the ingress of the sea. The situation was similar on all the islands.

Two-thirds of the population of Chowra was missing, presumed dead. Altogether, some 7,000 people in the entire island group lost their lives.

Satellite imagery and other such technological tools showed that the island had shifted its position by a few feet and had tilted towards the south by about the same amount.

Army rations for people affected by the flood

Relief camp outside DC's office

That inclination was enough to change the high tide limit by almost two metres. The water had come right up to the main road at some places, but nothing could be done about it.

For several days after the tsunami struck, hundreds of panic-stricken people awaited evacuation to the mainland. The jetty at Mus village was broken and could not take in ships. The smaller jetty at Malacca was broken too and was only fit for small fishing boats.

Although naval ships were near the islands within twenty-four hours, they were unable to find a safe berth to carry out any evacuation. The Navy did, however, get in the much needed food, water and medicines, which were transported to the island in smaller batches, using small naval choppers and rubberised boats, called Geminis.

This meant that the Air Force was the only means of immediate evacuation. The locals looked on from across the fence of the runway as the survivors at the IAF base made their first attempt to clear part of the runway for the first Dornier-228 aircraft to land, on the evening of 26 December.

Being a smaller aircraft, it could land on a shorter runway than the bigger aircraft. It brought in first aid, doctors and some water. It also evacuated the seriously injured to the hospital at Port Blair.

Clearing the runway had to be stepped up as the mighty IL-76 had to land to evacuate the families of Air Force personnel. The first IL-76 just about managed to land on the airstrip on 28 December, after the survivors with some local help had managed the Herculean task of temporarily clearing a larger part of the landing strip.

This plane, along with two An-32s, evacuated most of the Air Force and civilian survivors from Car Nicobar. How they managed to land and take off on such a short and damaged runway in the absence of any ground navigation and landing aids speaks very highly of the skills of our transport aircrew. For an IL-76, it was considered to be one of the riskiest landings attempted by our pilots. Kudos to their commitment to the cause.

In all, around 20,000 people were evacuated from the entire group of islands by whatever means available. Six thousand of them were taken to the mainland by air. Brave transport aircrew operated by night and day in very trying circumstances and used their superior flying skills to land and take off from the damaged runway. Sometimes, for night landings, the aircraft had to make do with only their integral landing lights since the emergency runway lights were not available at all.

One unit of Army Engineers moved in to help in the relief operations alongside the IAF and an Infantry Brigade. They were housed near the hangar, with the Brigade Commander

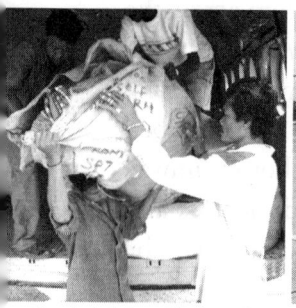
People helping with the rations

A Navy Chetak helicopter

Teamwork helped

The Navy brought in Gemini boats to transfer relief material from ships which could not dock

himself at the helm of affairs. These infantry men were sent out in small groups within and outside Car Nicobar for patrolling and to provide immediate relief.

They removed the road blocks and created new tracks and bypasses so that relief could reach all parts of the islands. They carried injured civilians to airfields and helipads for further evacuation. A few Infantry Combat Vehicles (tracked vehicles) were shipped in from the mainland and were very useful in traversing waterlogged and inaccessible areas.

The inaccessible areas had to be 'tracked', using duck-boarding and PSP sheets (perforated steel plates)—special material used by the Army to increase their mobility in treacherous terrain.

These tracks were to help us in being 'monsoon capable' for which enormous quantities of duck board and sheets of PSP were transhipped from faraway distances. Each kilometre of monsoon capable road thus constructed required either 1,330 PSP sheets or 800 duck boards. It was a mammoth task to transport this material from the mainland and install it on the island.

The Army also helped to strengthen the logistics chain, construct intermediate shelters and toilets, restore water supply, construct bridges and of course, provide the immediate first aid on site.

Makeshift kitchen in the early days

Day-to-Day Recovery

I OFTEN kick myself for not maintaining a diary of events, which would have helped me tell this story better. I had a laptop and wrote on it for a few days, but getting it charged was a problem and I had a huge load of work to get through. What little I had written on my office computer was also lost when the computer crashed. So, I had to draw on memories and images sharply etched in my mind when it came to writing this book.

During training, we are taught that the enemies of survival are—panic, fear, disease, thirst, hunger, heat/cold (remembered by the acronym PFDTHHC).

We were also taught to counter this by the logical priorities for survival, namely: protection, location, water, food and other aids (remembered by the acronym PLWFO). We could now practically understand the meaning and implications of each with the hows and whys of survival in our day-to-day life experiences.

In the first few days on Car Nicobar, we had to live in tents that had been erected by Air Force personnel on the parallel taxy track which was under construction for a year prior to our arrival. These were haphazardly arranged since they had been pitched in a hurry. Our first task was to get them erected in an orderly manner since this would be our quasi-permanent accommodation until we could move into something more solid.

Tents were pitched and temporary accommodation was created for officers and men under the open sky. The common mess tent was central to the living quarters and so was the medical tent.

Three large enclosures had also been erected earlier, next to the runway. One served as the Air Traffic Control and emergency command post, and the other two housed the communication equipment and makeshift hospital.

The regiment of Army Engineers that had arrived with their heavy equipment had to be accommodated within the base. They were given a part of what was once the football field, to set up their camp. We learnt a thing or two from the men in green as far as living in camps is concerned. These men were extremely good at innovation and we borrowed a lot of ideas from them to make our own lives comfortable in the initial days.

Living conditions were rudimentary and somewhat primitive in the early days. The bathing areas were right behind the tents where some tin sheets provided privacy.

Ops room and makeshift Air Traffic Control Room;
Early morning shave outside the tents (right)

Answering the call of nature meant a trip into the jungle armed with a bottle of water, a piece of soap and a shovel. At night, a torch and stick to spot and ward off inquisitive reptiles was also essential.

One functioning loo that had survived was in the Station Commander's office. Every morning we would hear him whirring off in his car to his office for his ablutions. He went off wearing his night clothes and would come back well-oiled, scented and dressed for the day.

Another washroom was discovered inside the station briefing hall that had been destroyed to a large extent by the earthquake, but the bathroom appeared serviceable. The drainage outlet, however, was blocked some way downstream, which meant the toilet would be serviceable only for a short while, but it was better than a trek into the jungle. One had to just clear a path through a lot of rubble and broken glass to gain entry to this luxury.

In a couple of weeks, we had the DTLs ready. DTL stands for 'deep trench latrine', an acronym used in military service from before the World Wars. It consists of a large trench covered with sheets of plywood with a gap in the middle. This was much more safe, hygienic and eco-friendly than jaunts into the jungle.

We used to jokingly refer to these DTLs as 'Thunder Boxes' and also joked about the possibility of the ply-boards giving way in the event of an earthquake!

After a few days of community living, we graduated to our own Officers' Mess tent, a bar tent and one shelter for guests. This was used by journalists who visited us during this time.

We slept under large-sized mosquito nets, impregnated with mosquito repellent, supplied by the World Health Organization. The mosquitoes were huge, and we often joked about being carried away by a flock of them and made a feast of, should we fall into a drunken stupor!

The fear of contracting cerebral malaria haunted us constantly. In the morning there was a black line of dead insects around our beds that had been killed when they came in contact with the medically treated mosquito nets.

To thwart the mosquitoes, we had an 'Odomos parade' before and after dinner. The tubes were carried along as an important part of our night rig to the mess too. The moment we came back to our tents after dinner, this parade continued. The lube-tube was passed around again before we slipped under the mosquito nets. In fact, some of us made it a habit to sleep with a tube under our pillows too!

There was a joke doing the rounds that an effective way of avoiding malaria was to drink two tots of rum before turning in so that the mozzies would be too sozzled to do much harm! Applying Odomos also ensured that we did not get bitten if a limb accidentally touched the net during sleep or a smart fellow managed to get into the net!

So serious was the malaria threat, that every Monday morning a parade was held to ensure everyone took their anti-malaria medication. The men had to line up and take

Three cheers to recovery

A makeshift bathroom under the blue sky

Cattle were unwelcome visitors to our tents

the pills right in front of the duty officer.

The local cattle were constant and unwelcome visitors. We had some water stored in our tents to help us in our morning ablutions. To get to this pure source of water, these animals literally tore into our tents and before you knew it, had their heads stuck into the buckets. Once they started drinking, no amount of shouting or prodding would make them budge.

To chase these fellows we had some bamboo sticks right next to our beds. The airmen would form big groups and would shout the animals away. Once, during one such shooing activity, these men were counter-attacked by a huge bull—the leader of the pack who we named 'Saandu' soon after.

We realised that these poor animals also required a source of salt-free water to drink and survive. We were impelled to create a water point for the cattle so that we could all live in some peace. Live and let live was an important survival lesson.

Survival was uppermost in our minds in those early days. We slept with a survival kit at hand, in case we had to evacuate in an emergency. This consisted of a pair of slippers, some money, a torch, some chocolates, a change of clothes, some medicines and the ubiquitous tube of Odomos.

The instinctive movement of animals towards the runway on higher ground was an early warning of an impending earthquake, as was the incessant chirping of birds. We also invented an early warning device that consisted of a weight hung from the ceiling with a small tin around it. When the earth moved, it would shake the weight and the clanging of the tin would say it all.

Minor after-shocks were quite common and didn't rattle

Medical aid tent

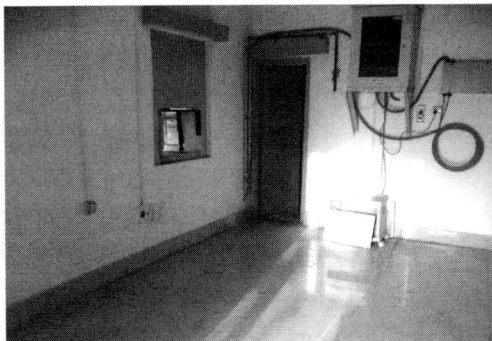

The office from where the author operated and lived during his stay

us. Up to five on the Richter scale was considered normal and we continued with our jobs, as if nothing had happened.

We experienced about 200 such shocks in the succeeding months that were above five on the scale. We did have a larger one sometime in March, post an earthquake centred in Sumatra, after which the first 'tsunami warning' was sounded. All of us gathered near the aircraft parking area and the survival orders were reiterated. Nothing happened, but we were able to go through a mock exercise nevertheless.

The most serious one occurred six months later, in July.

At about 9.30 at night we heard a loud bang and the earth shook more violently than ever before. We were finishing dinner in the mess and the light bulbs swung eerily. We ran out into the open and had to stand with our legs wide to stop ourselves from falling. The rumbling stopped after a while but the earth continued to sway. In a few seconds—which seemed like a lifetime—the shaking stopped and it was peaceful again.

The earthquake had measured 7.3 on the Richter scale. We got into our vehicles and went around the base, checking for any damage. Going towards the ocean in the darkness to check the coast was pretty scary to say the least considering the circumstances!

Airmen billets destroyed and after

We passed hordes of labourers who were rushing with their meagre belongings towards the runway, along with the cattle. The airmen too had quickly formed up and were moving to the runway in an orderly fashion.

The mobile networks were jammed and most of us couldn't get through to our loved ones. We managed to get through to Port Blair on our Air Force communications and learnt that a tsunami warning had been sounded.

We were prepared for such a contingency. Despite some panic and fear, our Standard Operating Procedure (SOP) seemed to be working. It was a busy night. Fortunately, the tsunami never came and we were back to the grind next morning.

It took me a few days to get my office going in what used to be the office of the Chief Operations Officer (COO). The broken glass and rubble was cleared, the bent fan was straightened out, and window glass replaced with pieces of cardboard and polythene.

A giant sheet of plywood was found and used as a partition to split the office space into a working area and a bedroom. It was quite some time before I could shift here from my tent, because there was no water and power supply to the building.

While the residential accommodation of the officers and men had suffered immense damage since it was located right on the beach, the offices, by and large, had been spared. The headquarters building had managed to survive despite flooding up to the first floor.

Once we had cleaned out these office buildings and a couple of barracks, they were used as residential accommodation as well as office space. The operations tent and the makeshift hospital continued next to the runway for a few weeks, till such time we could use the little balcony of the ATC tower as a command post and the lower floors of the building for the medical facilities and operations room.

The primary school, also right on the beach, had been completely destroyed by the tsunami and the brand new Kendriya Vidyalaya School building next door had been flooded, but managed to stand upright. This was cleaned sufficiently, and the building, minus its doors and windows, was turned over to the airmen.

They moved in somewhat reluctantly. On the first night, they came in a delegation to see me and said rather sheepishly that they were very uncomfortable staying so near the sea and wanted to shift back to their tents. They felt more secure staying close to the runway and together with the whole gang. I understood their feelings and gave them the green signal. They were back in their tents in a flash!

An Army Marches on its Stomach
Our diet in the initial days was a monotonous and basic *dal-chawal*, distributed from the large mess tent. Vegetables were in short supply. We managed to put together a collection of crockery and cutlery by scrounging around the island.

Washing up after meals was a problem due to shortage of water. I remember the men cutting up plastic water bottles

Crops and vegetation destroyed by the tsunami

to use as disposable plates—there was no shortage of plastic bottles.

There was so much work during the day that lunch was a hurried affair. But at night we sat in groups, had a drink and ate together to laugh our worries and stress away.

Shortly after we arrived, on 4 January 2005, Prime Minister Manmohan Singh visited the island for a few hours. He had to fly out in a small Avro aircraft from Port Blair, since the runway at our base was not big enough for his Boeing 737.

After he moved off in his cavalcade to meet the local population, I climbed into the aircraft to have a chat with the crew. I was treated like a hero by them and invited to have some interesting snacks and food. There were kebabs, cakes, biscuits, sandwiches, fruits and the like on offer. I was tempted to tuck in but thinking of my colleagues working hard down below, I requested the crew to spare as much food as they could for me to take back.

This was readily done and the food was brought to the

Snacking with the rescue team

Prime Minister Manmohan Singh visits the disaster site

hangar in large plastic bags. A shout for a fall-in and everyone assembled to feast on whatever was on offer. The sight of the boys enjoying the food and the feeling of sharing gave so much more satisfaction.

The rice and *dal* diet was quick and easy to cook and eat but it was monotonous, to say the least. A couple of days after our arrival, a Dornier aircraft from Port Blair brought in cooked puries in large baskets along with dry mashed potato *subzi* cooked by the wives of our men in uniform at Port Blair. It was a welcome change and the men looked decidedly happier that evening.

A fortnight later, we had the wherewithal to cook chappatis but restricted it to once a day since it took up a large amount of manhours.

Local fruits such as bananas, coconuts and pineapples came in from outside the camp. The locals gifted these to us in a goodwill gesture. Coconuts were plentiful but we didn't have the expertise to climb the trees. We contacted some young local boys who readily brought down the coconuts in exchange for some food and a tot of rum.

A friend in Chennai I was in touch with to get stuff for us and help us find good suppliers for our requirements, sent us a veritable feast one day. He and his friends were involved in relief work around the coastal areas of Tamil Nadu and so had a fair idea of what survival in a situation like ours meant.

After hearing my accounts of how we were managing, he put together a consignment of goodies provided by various good Samaritans, which included chips, nuts, sweets and huge plastic containers of pickles. It arrived, after some ingenious planning, on a plane carrying relief material. It was the first time we had tasted something sweet in days.

In the pre-tsunami days, perishables were stored in large freezers. The power breakdown post-tsunami meant that there was no means of preserving food. We received stocks of fresh vegetables and meat from Chennai in aircraft that flew in. But this was hand-to-mouth living.

Sometimes, an aircraft couldn't come in for many days due to bad weather, and it would be back to a frugal diet. Once in a while, the opposite happened and there was too much food. At times, birthday cakes were flown in from Chennai and sometimes, due to delays, we would celebrate with three or four cakes at one time!

Once the freezers got going, things improved. It was easy to understand the saying that an army marches on its stomach. With the kitchens producing good food, there was a quantum leap in the happiness quotient of the base.

The Japanese Well that had survived for more than sixty years was damaged by the tsunami

We soon had two kitchens, since the gastronomic requirements of the men and officers were different. In a few days, another new tent was erected to house a second dining hall so that our men could also enjoy their privacy.

Treasure Trove
The liquor cellar of the erstwhile canteen was discovered by our friends from the Army who were working alongside us. A large amount of liquor and soft drink bottles were buried under the sand. We had a good stock available with us till such time that we got our own from the mainland. As and when required, we would send a team of 'excavators' to dig it out for us.

The only problem was that the bottles had rusted seals and these couldn't be opened. The bottle had to be literally broken open and its contents passed through a muslin cloth which served as a sieve before being consumed. Some guys didn't mind a concoction of different flavours together!

Not a Drop to Drink
We didn't need a survival training course to tell us that water was an essential requirement for survival. Ironically, while liquor was not a problem, water was.

During the first few months, drinking water was in short supply. The only water point in the station was a well that was severely contaminated by the debris and sea water that had seeped into it. It was called the Japanese Well and had been in existence since the Japanese had occupied the islands during the Second World War.

It was fairly deep and we were told that it never dried up. Once we got it going, our daily requirement of one-and-a-half lakh gallons caused the level to drop by just six inches. This was naturally replenished in no time.

We surmised that the Japanese probably detonated plastic explosives or fired cannons into the soft earth to create such deep holes into the ground.

Normally, ground water is found at a depth of one metre in this area. This well was 35 metres deep! The jagged coral walls gave it a mystical look.

In normal times, the well had a natural way of filtering water. Water from the ground and the sea used to flow to this reservoir through the capillary action of the coral, which removed the salt content and the water was oxygenated too. Prior to the disaster, this well was a source of drinking water not only for the IAF station, but for some of the villages on the island as well.

The only way we could clear the now-polluted well was by siphoning out the water. In time, we acquired pumps and began pumping the water out.

Almost fifty to sixty thousand litres of water was pumped out every day by the engineers. Every week we sent a sample by courier all the way to Chennai to check if it was potable and waited with bated breath for the results.

Till such time this problem existed or sufficient quantity of water was brought in from the mainland, water had to be rationed. Only one bottle of drinking water was issued

Holding dearly to precious water bottles

to each individual on duty, including the various volunteer agencies like the police, Red Cross and other NGOs that worked alongside us.

One day, the situation became so critical that I had to make an emergency call to Delhi. Promptly the next day an IL-76 arrived with 40 tonnes of bottled water.

We were very happy to see it arrive. While offloading the packages, someone noticed that the water was well past its expiry date! After making inquiries, we got to know that this consignment had been lying in Delhi for quite some time.

Something was better than nothing, so we decided to use the water for everything other than drinking, including cooking. A call to the Vice Chief of Air Staff ensured that we got another 40 tonnes of good potable drinking water in the next couple of days.

It took four months to get the Japanese Well fit for use and the problem of water was finally resolved.

'Hello, Hello…'
Communication was another priority. It always is, especially during any calamity.

With no functioning mobile tower, mobiles were of no use. Basic landline communication was set up

The Station Commander makes the first call from a newly-installed STD booth

by the Army, with telephone wires running along the roads for local communication (which were often snapped by wandering cattle). We had two good satellite communication sets which were used to make contact with the outside world—mostly Port Blair and Delhi.

We used these to make our 'sitreps' (situation reports) and put in a word for items in short supply. It was a great feeling to be able to contact the bigwigs in Delhi directly and tell them what was required.

We allowed our men in uniform to contact their loved ones on the satphones. Staying in touch with their families was a morale booster for the men.

So 7 pm to 8 pm was 'welfare call' time. All personnel were allowed two calls per week for two minutes each. There was just enough time to enquire about members of the family. The men always assured their families that they were well and happy and there was nothing to worry about. Almost none of them could speak even for half the authorised time.

It would be almost six months before we could get reliable mobile and landline connections on the island. However, we did manage to get one STD connection going with much fanfare after a couple of months, but this was unreliable.

We had some basic ground-to-air communication sets with a range of about 25 miles. The communication sets required power and there was no reliable power supply for some time. Electricity on the island anyway was always supplied by huge diesel generating sets, all 6 of which had been completely destroyed.

Ravaged generator rooms

Day-to-Day Recovery | 61

New generators transported by helicopter

The 'motorolas' were constantly carried by all the important members of the team for constant and reliable short-range communication. This was one of the most important pieces of equipment we carried on ourselves all the time. Keeping these charged and serviceable was very important and was the responsibility of each member of the team.

We realised that reliable and instant communication was most essential in survival situations and ensured that this equipment was always kept ship-shape.

It took six months for new large-capacity generator sets, transported by sea, to be installed and provide uninterrupted supply. Till then, we managed with smaller sets of low capacity (the domestic variety) that had to be sparingly used.

So 'Lights out' was at 10 pm, barring weekends. Saturday, we splurged with an extended hour. One hour at dawn was sanctioned so that we could get out on the correct side of our beds and get ready.

We truly had a taste of what it must be like to live in parts of rural India where electricity was scarce.

With no competing city glare, there was plenty of moonlight to carry out basic tasks at night. But the dark nights of the waning moon were pretty disorientating. It was impossible to see even a few yards ahead.

Just how disorienting this could be I found out for myself. I was sleeping in my bed in my office one dark night when, through the swishing of the wind and the croaking of the frogs, I thought I felt the earth shake a little. It was about two o'clock in the morning. I got out of bed and headed towards the door, but walked straight into the wall!

Stunned, I sat down and looked for my survival kit. It was not under the bed! Panic set in. As my orientation improved and my eyes got used to the darkness, I realised that I had got out from the wrong side of the bed.

A little analysis brought me the answer. I usually slept with my feet pointing towards the door. That night I had gone to sleep the other way and hence the confusion upon awakening. We used this experience to explain to the troops how things can go horribly wrong with one small change in routine.

It was not just lack of electricity and drinking water that made us realise how slender our resources were. There was no store on the island from where one could buy even the basics. A small thing like a broken shoelace could become a big problem.

My sport shoes had a broken lace a few days after arrival and I had to request someone from the mainland to send me a pair. Until it arrived, I had to innovate with a string I found lying around.

One had to keep away from minor ailments too. A small cut could develop into 'cellulitis' in that high humidity; an upset stomach if not treated in time could land you into hospital at Port Blair 250 km away.

The most feared ailment, however, remained fever, which till diagnosed, was treated like cerebral malaria. The patient was on tenterhooks till the blood reports said otherwise.

Rebuilding begins!

Rebuilding Brick-by-Brick

THE WORK day started early on the islands. It is light in Andaman and Nicobar much before anywhere else in our country, being so far to the east. In fact, some of us used to talk about the need to follow a different 'eastern time' and reset our clocks by an hour or two. First light was at four o'clock in the morning and by the time we had breakfast, it felt like more than half the day was over.

In the first few days, the primary task was to clear the station of debris, identify the dead and give them a decent burial and commence the paper work.

During our early morning walks along the runway, we would identify target areas and deploy manpower to clear the debris. It was hard manual labour in the initial few weeks.

The Japanese Trail
Car Nicobar had a small ring road, approximately sixty kilometre in length which connected all the villages located along the shoreline. This was the only arterial connection for the district administration to look after its people.

Some books describe a road constructed by the Japanese (who occupied the island during World War II) that divided the island into two halves. This road had never been used after the War and had been reclaimed by the jungle. We unearthed this road link during our rescue efforts and used it to access the northern parts of the island.

Many young volunteers arrived from the mainland eager to help. One of them was an engineering student from Bangalore who stayed with us at the Army camp. Within a few days he was donning battle fatigues and roughing it out with us. He had intimate knowledge of the islands and was aware of the existence of the old road.

When the first patrols were launched to assess the damage to other parts of the island, he led the army troops through the foliage and discovered the long lost road.

Without this breakthrough, it would have been difficult for us to reach other parts of the island since the ring road was cut off at many places. The young man deserved a commendation for his selfless devotion to the rescue effort, but he left the island after a few days, his good work unrecognised.

A Japanese gun from World War II

Clearing Debris

Very soon we received some heavy earth moving equipment flown in on IL-76 aircraft and brought by sea. Other specialist vehicles like bulldozers arrived by ship from the mainland. We used to go down to the broken jetty at Malacca to receive these and help offload them from the ships. The day the ships arrived, almost the entire population of the station would head for the jetty in trucks, leaving behind only essential manpower for office work.

I remember one incident at the jetty during the offloading of a crash tender, a rather heavy truck which had been transported by sea together with other vehicles. We had a big enough crane for offloading, but the boom had to be extended to its full capacity to reach above the heavy truck due to the broken jetty. The strapping and securing was done, but the moment the weight of the truck came on to the boom, the rear of the heavy crane was hoisted into the air! We had a precariously balanced see-saw now.

The alert operator quickly lowered the truck on to the deck of the ship and averted a tragedy. The technical geeks then got down to plotting and scheming to get the monster off the ship. At one point we thought of sending it back to the mainland, but eventually a way was found to get the crash tender off the ship. Had the crane been lost to the waters, it

Hard at work at a construction site

would have created a major problem since it was an invaluable piece of equipment in the clearing and rebuilding process.

With the arrival of the bulldozers and JCBs (excavators), work speeded up and large tracts of the runway and roads were cleared of debris at a fast pace.

The water logging at one end of the runway continued despite our best efforts. Gas cylinders lay scattered around, presenting a fire hazard. They had to be moved to secure ground before we lit fires to reduce the trash to ash. There was no other way of getting rid of the trash; sending it back to the mainland was not economically viable or possible at that point in time. We, therefore, had no choice but to burn it. We were aware that this wasn't an environmentally sound method, but it was a Hobson's choice.

We called such 'burning' operations as 'controlled fires', with all hands on deck, ready with whatever equipment we had to ensure that the fire remained 'controlled'.

But Murphy did show his charm once in a while and create some unwanted panic. In one such incident, we had anticipated that the controlled fire would go towards an open area near the sea with the prevailing winds and die out.

Cleaning up the debris

Runway cleaning and debris removal

But Murphy decided to change the wind direction in such a manner that the fire now spread to the broken homes closest to the helicopter hangar. The fire was soon out of control and we had some spectacular explosions when a few gas cylinders ignited.

The fire now approached dangerously close to the hangars, forcing us to evacuate the helicopters and other equipment parked inside to safety.

Sometimes, stray dogs would help us find the dead, both humans and cattle, by fighting over their find. They were shooed away and an in-situ burial organised. We moved in groups of ten to fifteen members, armed with some shovels, axes, cameras and kerosene to burn bodies when found.

None of us had the guts to go near these bodies since they were in an advanced state of decay. The later we found the bodies, the more difficult it was to identify them. Photographs were taken. Items that lay next to, or on the bodies were also photographed to help in identification later by families and friends.

Occasionally, we found large quantities of cash and valuables next to the bodies. It appeared that people were trying to carry with them whatever they had of value to safety.

Vehicles arrive by ship

Burning and salvage operations

Hard at work

Besides this, various volunteers would find cash, jewellery and such valuables during the day at work and promptly deposit the same with us. These were stored in a strongroom in the Head Quarter building for some months till the inquests were complete. All unclaimed items were evaluated and used for making a 'Sarva Dharmsthal' at the base later.

C-in-C discussing with seniors

The Integrated Command

THE GOVERNMENT set up an Integrated Relief Command almost immediately after the tsunami struck, to coordinate all relief work for Andaman and Nicobar under the chairmanship of the Lieutenant Governor of the islands, Prof Ram Kapse. The Commander-in-Chief A&N was vice-chairman, operational head and spokesperson. The other members were a Member of Parliament, the Chief Secretary A&N Islands and one officer deputed from the Ministry of Home Affairs.

The state-level Disaster Management Committee of the civil administration had been instituted immediately

Inter-service interaction at the Officers' Mess

on occurrence of the tragedy, but the scale of the calamity needed a multi-dimensional and mammoth rescue and rehabilitation effort.

Besides the Armed Forces, 2,500 paramilitary, local and other state police contingents were involved in the relief operations, as also non-government organisations. Logistic cells were established at *INS Utkrosh* at Port Blair, Air Force Station Car Nicobar, *INS Kardip* at Kamorta Island and at the Coast Guard district HQ at Campbell Bay.

By the evening of 27 December 2004, the Integrated Relief Command (IRC) had some idea of the extent of the tragedy, although it was yet to get the complete facts and figures. This helped in the initial planning and execution of the relief operations.

The task and charter of the IRC was twofold: First, to mount an integrated relief and rehabilitation effort on the A&N Islands with special attention to the south Nicobar group of islands and aboriginal tribes. Second, to project all

A National Disaster Response Force team at work

requirements from various departments and ministries of the Government of India through the Ministry of Home Affairs.

Subgroups, called the Island Integrated Relief Organisation (IIRO), were formed at Little Andamans, Car Nicobar, Nancowry and Great Nicobar.

The search for survivors continued by land, sea and air for the next one month. At least one naval ship with a helicopter on board was available near each of the island groups, for immediate aid if required.

As many as 11,725 people were evacuated from the islands and around 8,500 received first aid in the first three weeks of the tragedy. This sustained, coordinated effort minimised deaths because of the availability of medical aid, food or shelter after the disaster.

Getting ready to take off: Inside the An-32 cockpit

Operation Madad

THE OPERATION launched for immediate relief was christened Operation Madad (Help). It lasted till 31 March 2005. It involved getting in loads of supplies by air and sea and distributing it among the islands.

A call for rescue

The aircraft parking area at Car Nicobar looked like a massive warehouse with tons of relief material lying around. This had to be unpacked and repacked into smaller packets for onward carriage by helicopters.

The local relief commissioner was supposed to be in charge of organising the re-distribution and was under immense pressure. We had to pitch in and help so that the loads went out in time, making way for fresh material.

A dedicated logistician was needed to organise the whole operation more efficiently but we had only one expert on base and he was busy with getting the base logistics going.

Excerpts from the diary of this Senior Logistics Officer,

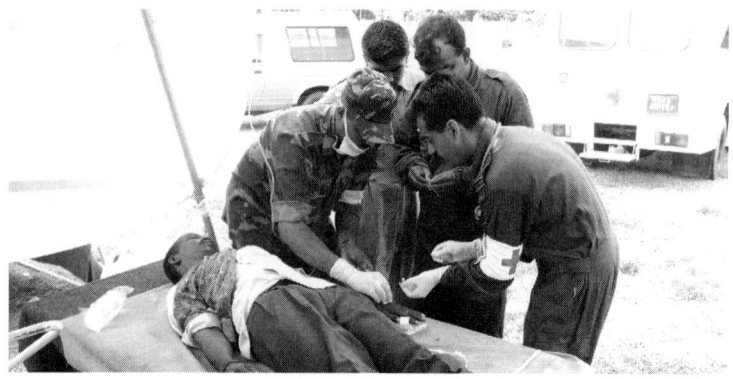

Treating the injured and the sick

Sqn Ldr Raja Mansharamani:

It was for the first time that I realised how complex and challenging it was to ensure availability of food, fuel, clothing and ordinance for a unit located in a remote area, so far away from the mainland. The complexities in supply lines not only were in multiple channels of demand and supply but also in the difficult working environment for all of us. The ultimate challenge was to transport these supplies from point of supply to the point of consumption—in time.

A total of 500 tons of relief was lifted by our choppers to various islands during this three-month operation. The fixed wing effort totalled about 700 tons. A total of about 9,000 people were evacuated by the pilots of the IAF.

The helicopters were also used to transport tons of text books, note books and other school material under the aegis of UNICEF and the Directorate of Education. This enabled the children on the islands to continue their studies and even appear for their board exams in March 2005. Farm equipment was also transported and this helped put agriculture back on its feet on these islands.

Heavy and voluminous loads like communication antennae, generators, ambulances and small vehicles were slung under the helicopters with nets and transported.

The Navy and Coast Guard put sixteen warships on duty. The challenge was to tranship essential supplies and people to and from the various islands

The Navy and Coast Guard put fourteen to sixteen warships on duty throughout the first phase of relief. They transhipped 2,800 tons of essential supplies and carried 5,700 people to and from the various islands.

Heavy engineering equipment, including fifty-seven vehicles, was transported by these ships in 109 sorties. *INS Brahmaputra, Rajput, Magar, Gharial, Sharabh, Darshak, Sandhyayak* and *Jyoti* and the Coast Guard vessel *CGS Sagar* were some of the ships that did yeoman service after the calamity.

It was important to get the jetties repaired before all the heavy equipment arrived. Army engineers were pressed into service and made temporary repairs and built improvised jetties so that ship to shore movement was easily accomplished.

The Public Works Department also pitched in with whatever had survived. Notably, a 'marine hard' (construction to facilitate swift offloading of vehicles and wheeled equipment on to the shore from landing craft that have the capability to come in close to the shore) was created. Beaching sites were scouted and identified and the special beaching vessels of the Indian Navy were utilised to land the loads on islands where berthing was not possible.

During this time, we had the excitement of a special guest landing at our base. The Queen of Nancowry was evacuated with her family from Kardip island. Some of us got our photos taken with the queen; the excitement was good for morale too!

Poachers

One night we received a panic call that there was some poaching activity reported from some of the islands north of Port Blair. We were told to come to Port Blair as early as possible the next morning to help in an operation to nab the culprits. On reaching Port Blair, an elaborate briefing was conducted for all stakeholders. Two helicopters were to take thirty-two marine commandoes and drop them on the little 'Landfall island' where the poachers were active. They had to move in at low level so as to have an element of surprise. Flying at deck level over the sea, they carried out a precision drop. Within no time they were called back in to pick up the commandoes and the apprehended culprits! I was part of this mission and the low flying over the sea was a fabulous experience.

Airlifts Continue

OPERATION MADAD was over by end-March 2005 but the task of conveying supplies to the various islands continued. A steady stream of aircraft flew in from the mainland. The An-32s brought in almost five tons of material whilst the giant Ilyushins were less frequent and brought in about 40 tonnes at a time.

This material had to be re-distributed by the choppers to various islands. The local administration told us the total load to be taken to each island and left it to us to plan our sorties.

Owing to the enormity of the operation and the fact that we were operating so far away from the mainland, there were pulls and pressures which led to decision dilemmas, further leading to some amount of confusion. This was well understood by us. Since we were the people closest to the scene, our decisions would naturally be in the best interest of the task at hand. We took them without qualms.

We received demands for assistance directly from different islands through our pilots. They got the latest news and requirements from wherever they landed. This helped all to plan better.

Offloading the material that came in by air and sea was difficult because we had no help whatsoever. Neither we, nor the local administration, could get any workers because there weren't any to be had, even for money. The islanders were preoccupied with getting their own lives and homes back on track. The loads had to be offloaded, segregated, stored and then distributed locally as well as to other islands.

Keeping Runway Fit

Since so much of the relief material was coming in by air, it was vital that the runway be in good shape. The surface of the runway was broken in many places and temporary repairs were carried out by filling the voids with sand and stones.

After every landing, a large amount of debris would come out of these cracks. We organised a quick reaction team to do the necessary filling of cracks after each landing so that the runway was available for further operations. Small mounds of stones and sand were kept along the edge of the runway to be used for this quick repair job.

Later, experts were flown in to assess the damage. They found that the surface was still good and only temporary repairs were required. Contractors were brought in with their repair material. The repair was carried out at night after

Keeping the runway in good shape was an important task and a laborious process

flying operations had ceased. Portable generator sets with adequate lighting equipment was locally fabricated to assist in the repairs.

At first light this special repair equipment was to be removed off the runway, the runway inspected minutely for any foreign object before we could allow any aircraft to use the strip.

It was a laborious process. Cracks were identified and marked with chalk. A diamond cutter machine then cut vertical grooves around and along the cracks to a sufficient depth. This resulted in a neat rectangular groove being created. After it was blown clean with blowers, a special black material mixed with resin went in. This dried quickly, after which finishing touches were given to remove the extra material at the edges.

Hundreds of such cracks were painstakingly filled over the months using forty-five tonnes of epoxy material to get the runway back in shape.

The heavy IL-76 aircraft stressed the runway the most. One night we had three IL-76s landing. The runway had to be repaired six times that night, once for each landing and take-off. Offloading continued throughout the night and it

Repairing the runway

was a back-breaking task. Hats off to the thirty-odd men who worked with passion and purpose and accomplished the task!

We had to take care of the crew of the transport aircraft too. They had to be made comfortable and we ensured that they got the much-needed rest after their long flights in their noisy machines. We never had a single complaint from any of these crews who were most understanding of our limitations.

Flight operations safety had to be kept in mind. With the number of human beings and vehicles wandering around the tarmac and the constant flurry of activity, this aspect had to be drilled into the heads of all operators and personnel on the tarmac so that safety was not compromised.

Briefings were carried out before the arrival of any aircraft and debriefs carried out after departure. I had to constantly be on the move to supervise so that no one let their guard down in these most trying of circumstances.

We did have one very unfortunate incident on the day the three Ilyushins were offloading. A load carrying vehicle brushed against the intake of the outer engine of the massive bird and damaged it. Although the damage was minor, the usual court of inquiry and paper work was an additional burden.

Rest & Recuperation

As we worked hard, we needed to play and rest too. In the beginning of our mission, there was absolutely no time to rest and recuperate. The work day was long and it left us with almost no energy to do anything else.

As soon as it got dark, we sat down to have a quick drink before dinner. Beds were pulled outside the tents to sit on and drinks came in plastic cups and mugs (glasses came in much

Picnics on the beach helped people bond well; on the way biscuits were distributed to local children

later). Chatting with one another in the dark, a few tots down our gullets, we were a cheerful lot.

On Sundays, things were more relaxed. We worked in civvies and could get up a little late. We worked like on any other day, but made time for some tennis ball cricket and volley ball. After a few days, we got a basketball court going and this game became a big hit.

The search for entertainment brought to light hidden talent among our own men. There were musical evenings with guitars, harmonicas and other musical instruments. As we settled into the months, our contacts in Chennai sent us the latest movies every week with the courier. We also saw movies and played games on our laptops— anything to take

our minds off the pressures we faced.

Some of the officers were yoga experts and we spent some time in the morning and evening learning and practising yoga and breathing techniques. This fitness routine helped us immensely health-wise and ensured that free time was spent fruitfully.

At times like this, it is easy for men to lose their way and get into bad habits, drinking, smoking or becoming reclusive. I am quite sure that if it weren't for the yoga and the outdoors, many of us would have succumbed to some ailment or the other.

After a couple of months, we had settled down sufficiently to begin exploring the islands and meeting the local people. Hours were spent sifting through and admiring broken corals. We also scoured the beaches for large-size shells and conches. The lucky ones did manage to find some extraordinary shapes and sizes which I am sure remind them of their stay on the island till date! Besides this, we often found human bones at all the beaches, confirming that the death toll had been very high.

We had one short stint of leave during the first three months. This was essential because the work was very stressful. A short spell of rest and recuperation worked wonders. The men returned with fresh minds and energy. They were transported to the mainland by the weekly 'courier' aircraft.

Going out was easy because the aircraft went back to Chennai almost empty. Getting back from Tambaram in Chennai, though, took much longer because incoming aircraft were fully loaded. One could go on a week's leave and come back after a month! Sometimes we had to requisition an additional aircraft to bring men back so that a new batch could get off.

I too managed a short stint of leave at the end of three

months. I was pretty tanned and had lost some weight which had everybody showing their concern. Returning to the noise and smoke of the city after several months away on a quiet island was a disturbing experience. Simple things like seeing a fan hung on the ceiling and water coming out of taps looked so strange!

Just three months of staying away from humanity had made a difference! Wherever I went, the talk was about how things were and how we had battled the aftermath of the disaster.

Back on the islands, the once treacherous beaches were now much in demand to while away an afternoon. Sometimes, the more adventurous amongst us planned long treks along the water's edge to far away beaches. We packed some chilled drinks and snacks along, with lots of biscuits to distribute to the children we met along the way.

The virgin sand and clear waters were most inviting and before long we were thoroughly toasted. We often spent time at the end of the day in an organised effort at beach cleaning.

The beaches of Car Nicobar had a notorious reputation because of the strong currents that carried off many a careless swimmer every year. We had one such tragic mishap ourselves, when one of our boys was pulled away by strong currents during an outing to the beach. It was sad to lose one of us; we were already dealing with a gigantic calamity and were confronted by another loss. We could not allow or afford to let it demoralise us because the task at hand was a mammoth one. We had to move on.

Devastation in the wake of the tsunami

Disaster on Show

A DISASTER of this magnitude invited what is called 'disaster tourism'.

There were the mandatory VIP visits that had to be facilitated. The visitors were taken to various 'spots' on the island and we explained the entire chain of events of the disaster. It was interesting to meet so many leaders whom we had only seen in print and media.

Some of the important persons who visited us during the first few months were the then Defence Minister, the then Agriculture Minister, the then Home Minister, the Chief Minister of Punjab, and the then Prime Minister and the then President. The Chief Minister of Punjab announced

Visit of George Fernandes

an additional Rs 1 lakh compensation for each of the Sikh families who had settled in the Campbell Bay area and had been displaced by the tsunami.

A large number of journalists descended on the island and they had to be provided accommodation and meals. The medical tent served as the visitors' room in the initial days. Many television programmes were aired on what we were doing and we achieved some measure of glory. I remember doing an interview while walking on the beach—a sort of 'walk the talk' with a journalist from a leading TV channel at the end of which I felt like a celebrity myself!

There was considerable good-natured one-upmanship amongst the Services about which one would get the maximum mileage out of the media coverage. Escort teams were positioned on the tarmac to pull in visitors for a briefing. We soon realised how frivolous this one-upmanship was and agreed to stop it.

An integrated media management team was formed, which ensured that all the organisations involved in the relief work got adequate media coverage.

It was always a mystery to me how the hordes of journalists managed to find transport to reach the islands. Without them, this story of determined rescue and rehabilitation would never have reached populations across the globe.

Initially, they were interested in reporting the devastation and speaking to the survivors. But in time, the line of reporting changed and focussed on how the islands were getting back to normal.

Most of the stories were positive, but some caused quite a stir in the civil administration as well as in political circles in Delhi. One understands why a good press is very important in such times, even if it is not one hundred per cent true. Negative publicity leads to lowering of morale of

Prime Minister Manmohan Singh's visit

the affected people, as well as the people who are involved in the rehabilitation efforts.

On the other hand, revealing the true picture allows for corrective steps to be taken and mistakes not to be repeated.

One episode highlights the power and reach of the press. At a press conference in my office, there were a large number of reporters. One of them was from Japan and spoke with the help of an interpreter. As I answered the numerous questions, the interpreter translated it into Japanese and the reporter typed away feverishly on his laptop. Later, over tea, I asked him how he would transmit his report to Japan. He floored me by saying that the press conference had been streamed live to Japan even as we spoke!

He had a small dish antenna connected to his laptop and placed outside the venue. Through this, he could transmit directly via satellite. People sitting in their homes in Japan were receiving a live feed while those in our own country got it after a day or two. We realised how important such reliable communication could be in disaster management.

The flow of journalists gradually eased off and the work of relief and rehabilitation also saw a marked slowdown. The next time we got media attention was when fighter jets began operating from the base.

The IAF's reach and capability to resurrect the base was beautifully covered by the print and electronic media.

The three Chiefs of the Armed Forces and many leaders were among the important visitors to Car Nicobar after the tsunami

According to official records available with the local administration, a total of eighteen international and ninety-six national media teams consisting of 230 media persons visited the islands in the first year.

There were many women journalists covering the events. One night, we had just got under our nets when I heard a commotion outside and a woman's voice arguing. I went out to see what the matter was.

The guard had stopped a woman from entering the tent area. I recognised her as a reporter from a well-known news channel. She wanted to stay in our camp for the night as she and her team had nowhere to go.

We made the team as comfortable as we could in the medical tent that had a few unoccupied beds. Although the mess had shut down for the night, some enterprising fellow went to the kitchen and managed to produce egg *bhurji* and bread for the famished crew.

Many years down the line, the journalist still remembers the good gesture of the IAF during her time of need!

We had another batch of female visitors from the Tata Institute of Social Sciences, who were involved in rehabilitation work in the southern islands. They were

A media briefing in progress

accompanied by their professor, a serving naval officer's wife.

We arranged for their transport to Katchal and Teresa islands by helicopter. How they survived there for the next one month, without proper food and shelter, is a story in itself.

Later, I read a research paper they had produced about their work and the issues relating to disaster management, which I found appropriate and interesting.

Accommodating women in a 'men only' camp had its problems. Although some women journalists did come and stay with us in the latter part of the year, in the beginning, we were not really 'lady ready'.

Part of the crew that flew in one day just within a week of our arrival was a woman officer in overalls. Many times, they would be part of the crew on aircraft that flew in and out of the base, so I enquired how her flight was and thought she would fly back when the aircraft turned back for the mainland in a few hours.

I was surprised to find her still around after the aircraft had departed. When we went in for lunch, we saw her at the table chatting with some officers. It turned out that she

An insurance agent assesses the damage

was part of the team that had come to install new radar equipment at the base.

The base did not have even the basic administrative support at that point to accommodate a woman officer. We discussed the issue and explained the situation to her. She, however, was ready to rough it out, young and bright officer that she was.

Since the base was not yet 'lady ready' like other operational bases, she was to return to the mainland. We assured her that we would be happy to have her back once we were more established administratively. We were sad to see her go but we admired her spirit.

Among other surprise visitors were agents of insurance and gas companies. The insurance agents had come to assess damage to personal property. They wanted proof that the cars and other insured property were actually destroyed! We found it amusing and made sure that these guys left as soon as they came in.

The gas company agents were there to take stock of assets like gas cylinders and accessories and wanted help in transporting them to the mainland. They had to furnish transfer vouchers to the survivors, based on this loss acceptance so that people could get fresh gas connections at their new places of residence. We showed them the extent over which gas cylinders lay scattered and expressed our inability to help them in the matter because we were busy with more important things.

On the first dawn after the tsunami

The Shock and the Survivors

STORIES OF survival, near-death experiences, and miraculous rescues kept coming in over the first few months.

When I was writing this book, I requested some of the survivors to give me a personal account. Even after so many years, most of them were reluctant to do so. I suppose no one wants to relive so tragic and traumatic an experience, or even think about it.

One of the most heartrending stories of loss was narrated by a young officer who lost both his children to the waters.

Here is his account of that terrible day:

We had all moved up to the first floor when the water level kept rising. A decision was taken to climb up to the top of the first floor, using the ladders that each house had. We didn't expect any water up there. As we sat there with our children and families pondering what would happen next, a huge wave suddenly formed in the sea and rushed towards us.

Before any of us could react, it just swept us from where we were. We were in deep water being pushed by the force of the wave. There was absolute mayhem and chaos. I could hear wailing ladies and children floating in the debris.

As I went under, I realised that I had my two small children stuck to me on both sides. My son was about three

Fallen cross of Jesus Christ

and my daughter was a toddler, barely a year old. I tried to paddle and get the children above my waist so that they could breathe. I was taking in some water too.

As I struggled to save myself and the children, I felt my little one going limp in my hands and slipping away from me.... In a couple of minutes my son too slipped away from me forever. I paddled feverishly and started looking for my wife whom I couldn't see anywhere. I was coughing and spluttering and trying to hold on to the debris that was floating with me.

I don't remember how and when I found myself clutching for dear life on to a plank of wood. This piece of wood got stuck to some fixed object due to which I didn't get washed away into the sea and I think that is what saved me.

After a while, when I could orientate myself, I tried to look for my missing children and wife in the debris. Since I had ingested some amount of water into my lungs, I felt weak and sick and collapsed.

My wife too was lucky to survive, thanks to a gas cylinder which she held on to and I saw her much later when I was in the makeshift hospital.

As I write this, I go through the agony of losing my two beautiful children to the wrath of the gods. At the same time, I am lucky to be alive and reunited with my wife and I guess that we shall have to rebuild our life once again.

Having ingested some amount of sea water, the young man was very ill himself and had to be evacuated. I met him a few days later, out of hospital and assisting the administration with paper work. Despite the huge loss he had suffered, he had his wits about him and was ready to get on with life. I was personally very proud of him. I had been his Commanding Officer not so long ago.

Miraculously Saved
About a week after the tsunami, we had a miraculous survival story. A little boy, barely twelve years old, came staggering towards the tents near the runway. Members of the media were waiting for an aircraft at the time and saw him. They rushed towards him and completely surrounded the frightened child, clicking photographs and bombarding him with questions. The boy was too stunned and weak to reply. He just collapsed in a heap.

Our medical team rushed to the rescue and brought the boy in. He was given first aid and immediately put on a saline drip. We cocooned him from the media for a few days till he was strong again.

He told us later that he had been washed away by the waves and found himself clinging to the top of a coconut tree. When the water receded, he was too afraid to come down and just continued to sit there. Stuck amongst the branches he found a big bottle of 'Sprite', which provided him the liquid he needed to survive. When hunger and weakness got the better of him, he slid down, scratching himself all over.

A Baby is Born
We were also told of the rescue of the pregnant wife of one of our airmen, from the third floor of her house. She was in an

advanced stage of pregnancy and stuck atop her house since the lower half had been washed away. A group of airmen tied bed sheets and curtains together and rescued her to safety in true 'filmy' style. She was evacuated to the mainland soon after and delivered a healthy baby at Chennai.

Braveheart
Meghna Rajshekhar's story of survival is even more intriguing. The 13-year-old daughter of an IAF officer lost her entire family to the waters.

She was sucked into the sea by the receding waters but found a broken door floating by and clambered on to it to stay afloat. She had no clue in which direction lay land. She floated on the ocean, fighting fear and panic. She narrated how she waved out to airplanes that flew overhead and was threatened by sea snakes. Badly bruised, but alive, she was fortunately washed ashore two days later, on 28 December 2004. The base arranged for her immediate evacuation to the mainland. She is reported to be living with relatives and is a grown young woman now.

Meghna Rajshekhar at the memorial function, one year later

Bridge destroyed

There was the rescue by helicopter of seventeen marooned people at Katchal island in the first week after the tsunami. The helicopter hovered above and each one was winched up to safety, an operation that required superior flying skills.

There were the doomsday prophets too. A doctor from Bangalore was part of the rescue effort in the initial days. He was a good storyteller and the men would gather around him every evening to hear his tales. He told them how the island had become weak due to the earthquake and the 'stem' holding the island afloat would soon give way, and it would then sink to the bottom of the ocean!

Word of this impending catastrophe spread quickly and the next day a large number of men applied to go home on 'emergency leave'. I soon got to the bottom of things and realised who the culprit was. The doctor got his marching orders, but it took us much time and effort to convince the men that the danger was a figment of the doctor's imagination.

Some who had lost their loved ones, kept returning to the islands at regular intervals in the hope of finding them. They were told by soothsayers and *jyotishi*s that their kin were still alive and surviving in a particular place or island. We didn't dishearten them and did all we could to help them but it was all in vain.

Operation Samman

One rather unusual rescue operation we mounted was not of a human being, but of a statue. It was named 'Operation Samman'.

In May 2005, we were assigned the task of finding and rescuing the statue of the late Prime Minister, Indira Gandhi, which had been installed at Indira Point which is the southernmost tip of the islands (and of India). The waves had washed it away.

When exploration by ground parties proved fruitless in locating the statue, an aerial search was initiated. One day, whilst carrying out a routine sortie during low tide, the pilots spotted something that vaguely resembled the bust, embedded in the sand and slush. A ground party was immediately despatched and the finding confirmed.

Hauling the eleven feet tall and six feet wide statue weighing 1,500 kilos to land was no easy task. Marine commandos were dropped near the area. They carefully dug out the statue and removed the sand inside the hollow of the bust to make it as light as possible. The statue was then dragged to an open space from where a hovering helicopter winched it up. It was slung under the helicopter and transported to Campbell Bay about twenty minutes flying time away.

When the helicopter landed with its cargo intact, there was much cheering and backslapping. It would be another couple of years before the statue was reinstalled.

Jaguar taking off

Op Ready

WE WERE standing on the tarmac, excitedly waiting to receive the six fighter jets that were being flown in from bases on the mainland. The advance party of fighters with associated equipment had flown in on 6 April, exactly 100 days after the tsunami struck and all but destroyed the Car Nicobar Air Force Station.

11 APRIL 2005
We had promised the Chief of Air Staff Air Chief Marshal SP Tyagi at the beginning of our mission that we would be ready to take on all operations within 100 days. And now, D-day had arrived. The primary task of cleaning up was done, the runway repair carried out and the basic environment for safe conduct of operations had been created.

The six fighters from IAF bases on the mainland would be flying for eight hours non-stop to reach our base. They would be given mid-flight refuelling by IL-78 tankers thrice during the journey. We had to ensure a very clean runway and parking slots. A grand reception ceremony was planned for 14 April, with the Chief of Air Staff as the chief guest.

It was an important day for me and I was a bit nervous. I flitted about the station, checking on the arrangements. As

Air Chief Marshal SP Tyagi interacts with Air Force personnel

the first aircraft approached to land, I parked myself in the air traffic control, armed with binoculars and a video camera.

Our hard work had come to fruition today. The base was truly 'fully operational'! Along with the fighter detachment came a lot of goodies sent by our families from the mainland as also the families of the visiting squadrons. It was a week of celebrations! We felt so wanted and important, with all those sweets and good wishes we received!

The fighters stayed for a week. It was good to interact with the crew and tell them our survival stories. They were clearly impressed with us and what we had done. We received a pat on the back from the Chief of Air Staff. In the true spirit of 'Jointmanship', the CAS asked the Commander in Chief, Andaman Nicobar Command, Lt Gen Aditya Singh to address the press conference at the end of the fighter flypast, done in honour of the base. We also heard of these flypasts being done over radio broadcasts, just like it used to happen in the early eighties!

For the short while they were there, Car Nicobar felt like

a normal IAF base with hectic flying activity, lots of noise associated with fighter jet flying and some good partying too. We were sad to see the fighters fly back to the mainland a few days later.

Air to air refuelling of the Jaguar; Photo op with the sleek SU-30 MKI (below)

Rising like a Phoenix

WE BEGAN working on our next goal almost immediately—receiving the three Service chiefs to mark the first year of the tsunami. It was a long way off but a lot needed to be done as the rehabilitation phase was now in full swing.

The first changeover of staff took place end-March, beginning of April. The first lot of personnel, who came in immediately after the tragedy, were sent back to their units. We needed more permanent tenures now, since the pace of work had caught on and needed better supervision.

Since the living environment was still difficult, Air HQ was of the opinion that we must get a fresh lot of hands on deck every three months for the first year. After that, it was to be a one-year tenure for the next two years; and by that time the station would be on its feet and a normal 'field tenure' of two years would follow.

The VIP guests who visited us during the time were so mesmerised with the beauty of the place despite the mass of destruction all around, that they would often quip, 'Why does anyone want to have a restricted tenure here? This is an ideal place for a honeymoon!'

The troika heading the three 'pillars' of the station—the Chief Operations Officer (me), Chief Administrative

Admiral Arun Prakash (CNS) and Air Chief Marshal SP Tyagi (CAS)

Officer (Wg Cdr Sandeep Johri) and the Chief Engineering Officer (Wg Cdr Dipak Lahiry)—volunteered to stay on for a full year. We had started many projects together and we wanted to see these bear fruit. We also felt that in the larger interest of the service and to ensure continuity, it was best that we stayed on.

Our men regarded us with more than just respect for volunteering to stay on. But I must admit that we were quite enjoying the challenge, despite the hardships.

We also learnt a lot about the need for better planning of relief material, if precious resources were not to go to waste. Some of the relief items that came in were of no use to the local population. They promptly sold it off to contractors at whatever price was offered. The contractors, subsequently, shipped it to the mainland and sold it for a hefty profit. We got to know that this material was then shipped back to the mainland as more relief material!

We received a lot of food grains and other perishables for distribution to other islands. Sometimes, we found the stuff rotten and unfit for human consumption. Along with the food grains came big rodents. We had to be careful to exclude

these creatures when we loaded the aircraft, as just one rodent could chew away wires and cables in the helicopter and cause an unnecessary problem in flight.

My bugbear was the amount of paper-work involved in everything. Dull and monotonous though it was, it was nevertheless important and had to be done. If anything had to be bought or any infrastructure created, in fact, if a single penny had to be spent, it was preceded by paper-work. Approvals had to be sought and tenders invited. All this had gestation periods, which were irritating and time consuming. But we realised that procedures must be followed and quickly learnt to do it meticulously.

A big chunk of paper work involved the boards of inquiry into losses, both human and material. This was an essential exercise. If the inquests were not done in time, compensation to the next of kin would be delayed, causing further agony to the bereaved. Material losses had to be legally written off so that new stuff could be ordered against the deficiencies created. This had to be done diligently since it involved legal issues, and could lead to long standing complications. In time, we had enough computers and computer savvy staff available on the base to get this done.

A visit by the then President of India, Dr APJ Abdul Kalam

Supreme Commander Comes Calling

SOON AFTER the base received the IAF fighter contingent, we had to prepare for the visit of the President of India, Dr APJ Abdul Kalam.

On 2 May 2005 we received intimation that the Supreme Commander of the Armed Forces, along with his entourage, would be visiting us on 6 May. We rushed to get the base neat and tidy for his visit and prepare two of our helicopters ready for the President.

VIP seats and carpets were flown in from the mainland and the helicopters decked up for the occasion. Just a day before, one machine developed a snag. More hard work was called for, and seats removed and re-fitted in a hurry.

Tea with the President

The weather gods were not happy. It rained, and the President was unable to fly to other islands as planned. He changed his programme and drove around the island and met the locals. He also found time to have high tea with us which was arranged in the hangar.

A very popular figure, President Kalam was keen to talk to the men. We were thrilled to be speaking to the man himself and posed for photographs alongside him. One of the men explained how hard life was on the island. The President asked what would make life easier. Our smart aleck replied that if we were granted a special allowance, it would be a big motivating factor!

The President asked his Military Secretary to make a note, and assured us that we would soon hear from the government.

And true to his word, we had an additional 25 per cent of our pay warming our bank accounts in a short time.

The weather improved on the second day and President Kalam made an aerial survey of the islands to the south. After he left, we had a two-day break to unwind! We organised a full-fledged conch hunting competition, along with a picnic to one of the beaches that we rarely visited.

Celebrations

We always looked forward to celebrating all kinds of occasions, be it birthdays, anniversaries, or any happy circumstance. This was important since it got us together at the social level and kept us occupied and alive to each other. Besides this, all kinds of festivals were celebrated with gusto.

On the day of the Onam festival, the army engineer troops, who were from Kerala, invited us over for a meal. The quality and different dishes that were prepared by them left us astounded and also taught us a thing or two about innovation!

A traditional meal served on plantain leaves was the highlight of the day and we gorged ourselves silly. Other festivals like Holi and Diwali got the whole station celebrating together.

Celebrating Onam

When the Commander of the base, Group Captain Dhar, turned 50 we decided to give him a surprise party. An entertainment programme was organised which would have given Bollywood a run for its money.

Each of the celebrations at night was accompanied by a nice big bonfire. Although too hot to sit anywhere close to it, it certainly helped in getting the celebration going.

All pilots were supposed to undergo 'dinghy drill' training on a periodic basis to train for sea survival. It involved the pilots being dunked into water and then winched up by a helicopter.

One also had to practice using the Mae West and the dinghy—both crucial requirements for survival at sea. Almost all these training practices were done on a holiday and ended up in a nice picnic at the beach, with the others joining in after the training module was completed.

A new lot of people meant settling down to a new set of group dynamics. We needed to gel with each other fast and get organised as a team to work together. This team was broken to a large extent every time we had a change of crew. We, as the permanent incumbents, had to get this group cohesion going and extract the same work output that we did from the earlier lot.

We had to also motivate the few who had heard all the wrong things about life on the islands. We had to get these guys to dispel their myths and get to move on at the earliest.

There were no working hours or no working uniform as such. The mantra and motto seemed to be 'Just Do It'!

Astro navigation and star gazing also became popular when some of us procured some good telescopes. The clear skies and the clarity of the atmosphere were ideal for star gazing.

Some of the youngsters spent time playing pranks on each other, draped in white bed sheets in the middle of the night. Sometimes it worked, but most of the time the people were so tired and caught up with sleep that they wouldn't be bothered even if it was a real ghost.

Sometimes, it is good that people are forced into playing games and use some of their spare time to be with people. The commander was a keen sportsman and he wanted each one in the station to be present for games every evening, once we were settled in. While some resented this at that point in time, it was a good thing to do for self-preservation.

We also managed to play a large number of football and volleyball matches with the local villagers. Since the base was the only place where the grounds were brought up to playing standards initially, we had a large number of locals who would come and practice their games in the evening inside the station premises. This prompted us to organise some friendly matches on a regular basis. This also helped in building trust and bonhomie with the local population.

A large number of our men used to spend the evenings together at the local prayer hall, which had all the gods under one roof. A *dholak* and harmonium would appear in the evenings and freshly oiled and powdered men spent time singing hymns and popular religious songs, prior to dinner.

This again ensured that people were together and always in touch with each other—so important in a situation like this.

Beach cleaning exercise

Constructing the new temporary houses

Rehabilitation

BY JUNE 2005, six months after the disaster, the first part of the rescue and relief operation was over. We were getting into the rehabilitation phase now.

A quick look at the cold statistics will show the extent of the damage, and thus, the extent of the task of rehabilitation that had to be undertaken.

Cold Numbers

The IAF lost 116 personnel from the Car Nicobar base, for whom compensation was paid to the next of kin. Those declared 'missing, presumed dead' required more paper work to be completed.

The cost of damage to buildings and installations at the base was estimated at Rs 38 crore. These had to be the 'written off' charge of our records. Other material losses in terms of personal property were estimated at Rs 15 crore. The disaster caused a loss of about Rs 150 crore to government property on the base. These losses had to be certified by a board of inquiry and written off so that fresh acquisitions could be made.

In the entire island group, a total of 10,000 households were affected by the disaster which amounted to around 60,000 people being displaced.

In Car Nicobar, according to official estimates, 400 persons were identified dead and around 3,100 were reported missing, presumed dead.

Out of 5,300 hectares of total farmland available in the district, farmers permanently lost about 2,200 hectares of cultivable land besides large tracts of beaches inundated by the sea.

About 40,000 hectares of forest land was damaged on the Islands. Some 17,000 houses were damaged and 10,000 completely destroyed. A total of 160,000 livestock perished in the waters.

Eighty-five schools were completely destroyed and thirty-five health centres were washed away. Power capacity of 37 megawatts was destroyed too.

Twenty-four jetties were severely damaged and required major engineering efforts to become serviceable.

The government erected about 7,000 shelters, almost 4,000 on Car Nicobar alone. Most were provided with electricity, flooring and water.

Electricity for other villages on the islands is still a major issue due to the slow progress of road construction. However, all the fifteen villages on the Island of Car Nicobar are connected by black-top metalled roads today.

Our logistics in-charge, the smart, young Squadron Leader Raja Mansharamani was always smiling and helpful. He and his team salvaged large amounts of equipment from all parts of the station and brought it back to use.

This equipment had been written off by an earlier inquiry. By salvaging so much equipment, he saved the exchequer about Rs 66 lakh. It was a job well done.

Good logistics ensured that we were never short in terms of food, clothing, fuel, spares and the like. As COO of the base, I was required to be in constant liaison with logistics so that the incoming loads were prioritised, as all stakeholders felt that their load was the most important and needed the highest priority.

I think we managed fairly well. The major discussions over dinner at night were about who and what was to travel in the next incoming aircraft. These discussions created a strong bond that continues today.

Since almost everything had to be built from scratch, the amount of planning was colossal. We had to site the new accommodation which was to come up in porta-cabins. These are lightweight structures prefabricated in the factory on the mainland and brought to the island in bulk by ship and air. These had to be bolted together to form our new homes. The first 14 porta-cabins, along with the internal and external fixtures, cost Rs 2 crore. They were erected on cement plinths which had to be built first.

For quite some time we did try to get some additional land allotted to us to site the new living accommodation on a high feature, almost adjacent to the Air Force land. Despite the government being convinced, we couldn't get them to convince the local village elders to heed our request.

On these islands, the ownership of land rests with the tribes. The tribal leaders were the ones who argued that the total land available for their own requirements had been reduced and, therefore, they were not in a position to allow us any more land on the island. With this status quo, we had to perforce squeeze ourselves on whatever spare land we had and also scale down our plans to have a family accommodation project.

A most welcome addition to our living conditions were the new toilet blocks. New generator sets, gymnasium infrastructure, furniture, modern kitchen amenities, curtains, carpets… they came in as we slowly and steadily marched towards becoming a full-fledged operational base.

As we came towards the end of the year, we started allowing some families to visit the base for short periods. The newly married lot was very happy to get their spouses to the island and boast of what had been achieved! Along with the wives came children during the winter vacations—although for a short time, and the base did finally look like a normal family station!

The families were treated like VIPs and shown around the island by all of us. Some of them reciprocated by taking over the mess for an evening and cooking us some delicious meals which was a change from the usual.

To put up all this infrastructure, labour was needed from the mainland. The daily wage was almost double that on the mainland, with free food and lodging provided by the contractors.

Some of these big contractors hired an entire commercial aircraft to transport the men in and out of the islands. They also made arrangements for them to be sent home for well-deserved breaks during festivals. Contractors could afford all this because they made pots of money—charging at least three times what they would for work on the mainland.

All this labour had to be housed in camps inside the station and their health and hygiene requirements attended to. We had to constantly be after the contractors to maintain cleanliness and discipline among their labour force.

Civil, paramilitary and military agencies as well as voluntary organisations worked together. Given the peculiarities of these islands, there was no alternative but to synergise all efforts to provide quick and efficient relief, rehabilitation and development.

The Integrated Relief Command first set up by the government in the immediate aftermath, to coordinate relief work, was wound up on 21 July 2005, but all agencies concerned continued to work together thereafter. This bonhomie and synergy among the agencies had a major role to play in the resurgence of the A&N Islands.

In the words of Admiral Arun Prakash, former Chief of Naval Staff and chairman, Chiefs of Staff Committee:

While paying solemn homage to those who gave their lives in the tsunami disaster, I express admiration for those who have resumed the business of life with courage and fortitude.

New Porta-cabins for airmen

The Memorial

The Memorial

THE COMMANDER-in-Chief of Andaman & Nicobar Command Lt Gen Aditya Singh wanted a memorial to be built at the airbase to commemorate those who had perished in the tsunami. He asked his Chief Engineer to design the monument around the theme 'Perpetuity'.

The design incorporated the Obelisk of Tuthmosis, the Egyptian Pharaoh, dating back to 1500 BC. The outer walls were fashioned along the lines of the Sanchi Stupa dating back 2,000 years.

The monument was built in the eastern corner of the base, right behind the HQ complex. It comprises a red stone base on which a 22 feet yellow stone obelisk stands (that was the maximum height of the tsunami wave at that point, we were told). This stone, weighing 35 tonnes, was flown in from Delhi in an IL-76 and required super-human effort to be erected with the limited resources available.

A huge metal eagle sits atop this obelisk and faces the ocean, indicating alertness and resilience of the IAF base. The front panel faces the direction of the first tsunami wave to hit the island, and dedication plaques adorn the gate posts of the memorial. From conceptualisation to completion, the monument took three months.

Three Service Chiefs, JJ Singh, Arun Prakash and SP Tyagi, at the memorial service

A memorial service was planned for 26 December 2005, on the first anniversary of the disaster and preparations had to be made to host this important event.

The Commander-in-Chief of Andaman & Nicobar Command, Lieutenant General Aditya Singh personally monitored the progress of the memorial and his frequent visits ensured that the base was up to inspection standards well in time for the inaugural function. Tri-service bands were flown in and we enjoyed some melodious evenings listening to them practising.

I was now on my way out to my next exciting assignment—to the United Nations Peace Keeping mission in the Democratic Republic of Congo (DRC). Organising the inauguration of the Memorial was to be my last task on the island. I was to leave the islands after the ceremonies were over, in the special aircraft that would take the guests back to the mainland. In fact, my farewell from the station was planned for the night previous to the inauguration. I did feel a tad sentimental leaving the base.

The ceremony was a sombre affair, with all the three Chiefs in attendance. The next of kin of all those who perished were invited to be present.

Before the formal salutations and respects were paid, the three Chiefs jointly unveiled the monument and dedicated it to the airbase. The guests planted saplings all around the complex. Today, all these saplings have grown into a nice thicket of trees.

The ceremony was also attended by the Chief Secretary of the Andaman & Nicobar Islands as well as a large number of high ranking officials from the military and civil establishment. Media teams were present in large numbers; this time we had the wherewithal to transmit the ceremony directly to viewers on the mainland.

The highlight of the event, which left many of us teary-eyed, was the tribute paid by the tsunami survivor Meghana Rajasekhar. She was among the first to lay a wreath at the monument along with some next of kin of those who perished.

The occasion was a fitting finale to my stay on the islands.

Tri-Services Guard of Honour at the unveiling of the memorial

Honourable guests arrive for the ceremony

Attendees at the memorial ceremony

In Memorium

FOR MANY years after my year-long posting at Car Nicobar, I kept jotting down my experiences of that seminal year. Every time some event triggered my memory, I wrote it down on a notepad headlined 'tsunami'.

The memories are still fresh and etched deep. When I finally decided to put it all down as a record of what had happened and what was achieved during one of the worst natural disasters to strike our country, I realised it was not difficult to recall those days.

These memories will soon fade and the writing be forgotten. But I pray that we don't have to go through another tragedy of this magnitude ever again.

This book is a tribute to the valiant men and women who stood tall against all the odds to help resurrect the Islands of Nicobar. The IAF is, undoubtedly, proud of them for resurrecting this important base, while at the same time assisting in the rescue, relief and rehabilitation efforts in the Car Nicobar Islands.

Then Flying Officer DJ Bhandarkar put it well when he wrote in his diary:

Despite personal injuries and having lost our belongings, we stood up as one and faced the disaster in the true

The author with Station Commander Carnic

traditions of the Armed Forces of 'Service before Self.' I count myself fortunate to be a part of all this; that I could stand up when demanded and hold my ground as an Air Warrior.

This book is also a tribute to those who lost their lives, and to the survivors who lost part of their lives to the violent ocean on that fateful day. The destruction of life and property, the upheaval and uprooting of so many lives was such an intense experience that it changed the way many of us look at life.

The aftermath, though, was also important. Rebuilding and reorganising was an integral part of the experience. I would often quote this proverb during my talks to young airmen:

'Life is like a grindstone; whether it grinds you down or polishes you up; depends on what you are made of.'

It is my firm belief that living through the aftermath of the tsunami was our grindstone. All of us were polished to perfection by the experiences we went through in that period.

Déjà Vu

At the end of 2013, when I had almost finished writing my story, I decided to make a quick trip to the islands to get some statistical data and to refresh my memory of the days spent there.

It was a clear morning as we approached the island. I was quite excited and as the island came into view, I craned my neck to see it, just as I had done nine years ago. I was off the small plane and on to the tarmac at Car Nicobar as soon as the engines fell silent.

Waves of memory washed over me as I stood on the tarmac and looked around me. I wanted to bend down and kiss the earth at my feet, but I thought that would appear too melodramatic to the people who had come to receive me.

I spent the morning talking about what it had been like and what we had done. The tragedy was largely forgotten and mentioned mostly in files and presentations now. On the day of my arrival, the airbase was, coincidentally, going through a mock disaster management exercise.

It was stimulating to see what the present practices and standard operating procedures were and I was more than happy to render expert advice! I had my time in the sun that day as I went around telling our story and seeing the bewildered faces of people who could not even imagine the destruction wrecked on the very same airbase.

The station was neat and clean like in the pre-tsunami days. What was different was that there was no sighting of the sea from any point at the base, even though the roar of the waves crashing against the shore was audible.

The old abandoned homes had been razed to the ground and the debris buried deep underground, forming a big mound along the shore. Along this bund were planted casuarinas and coconut trees in neat rows. These had almost grown 20-30 feet high. This tree-topped mound, it was hoped, would act as a buffer should the ocean's fury ever recur. Ironic that the wreckage caused by one tsunami, should be used to stop another.

What was shocking was that the beautiful beaches along the base were almost completely gone, taken over by the sea. It

In the aftermath of the tsunami, the beaches lost their beauty and allure

was difficult to imagine that so much land had been virtually eaten away. The high tide line now came in well beyond the spot where the first line of houses existed. Debris from those times still lay strewn along the beaches in some places.

As I went from village to village on the island I saw more evidence of the nine-year-old disaster. Large amounts of debris still lay scattered along the tracts of marsh land that had formed then. There was the familiar smell of salt and rotten wood, taking me back in time. I realised that it was near impossible to get all that rubble and marsh cleared ever.

I also saw and drove through some of the villages abandoned from those times—they looked so ghost like. While doing so, I bumped into some enterprising young men from Kerala who had established a small bakery and eatery in one of the abandoned homes.

Normal life has since returned to the islands, Chief Captain Aberdeen Blair told me when I went to meet the octogenarian. He looked in fine fettle and remembered the days of the tsunami and the aftermath with reasonable clarity.

Schools and churches are back on their feet and agricultural activity is in full swing. The population has taken to growing vegetables in larger quantities

today. Just a fraction of it is sold in shops; most of it is consumed by the local people or used for barter as in the earlier days.

I went to meet the District Commissioner in her office who told me that people had gone back to their usual lives now.

A disaster that changed so many lives is not so distant that people don't remember it. A study of the psychological impact of the tsunami, conducted by a well-known institute, amongst the adult populace of Nicobar showed that 70 per cent of the population of the islands feared the sea and didn't venture into its waters to earn their livelihood. About 73 per cent said they did not fear the tsunami and 27 per cent felt that the tsunami would strike them again.

The study goes on to say that the tribal population was found to be more resilient. The disaster didn't significantly change the way they lived and looked at life. They do remember their loved ones, but have been able to get on with their lives. The tragedy, therefore, hasn't had any perceptible psychological impact on them.

Their resilience, in my opinion, owes to the joint family system and the practice of community living. They don't believe in accumulating wealth or property. I was told that they don't have a word for 'widow' or 'orphan' in their language.

As I drove along the ring road I saw two State Transport buses crossing each other, going in opposite directions. These were the only two buses on the island even nine years back, showing that public transport had not improved. But the numbers of two and four-wheelers had increased and were parked haphazardly as is the case everywhere in our country.

I noticed signboards along the road advising people in case of an earthquake to stay away from the beaches and head towards higher ground.

I paid a visit to the tsunami memorial at Big Lapathy village and offered my prayers. This memorial was built in 2006. Photographs of the tsunami devastation and the rehabilitation work thereafter are displayed in little huts around the mounted granite slabs that bear the names of all the deceased.

Although not very well-maintained, it is a reminder for the islanders of what happened here and how their resilience helped them to recover as a community.

Station Commander, Group Captain Sanjeev Vashishth in his office

The author (left) with the Chief Captain of Car Nicobar Island

At the Air Force base, I found time to spend a quiet ten minutes at the IAF memorial, praying to God to spare this pristine natural habitat the next time. The Commander showed me around a Sarva Dharamsthal that had been built and managed by the security personnel.

I sat down on the floor and closed my eyes in silent tribute to all those who had perished. The silence, except for the roar of the sea and the sound of the wind in the trees, had a calming effect. I walked out with moist eyes.

Except for the debris peeking through the thick undergrowth, the only reminder of the tsunami at the IAF base is the school building complex. It still shows signs of damage, though I was informed that it was to be repaired and used again.

The airbase will soon have a modern gymnasium, swimming pool, new Officers' Mess cum bachelor accommodation, shopping plaza and other infrastructure available on any modern airbase.

What it will not get in the foreseeable future is family accommodation for the men; the base will continue as a 'field-area'.

For the local population, the government has built some wooden homes on stilts and I visited one such 'model' home of the Chief Captain. The old igloo-style homes were nowhere to be seen, except for a traditional one at Chukchuka village. These traditional igloo-style homes were already going out of fashion before the tsunami. Many were situated close to the sea and washed away; and no one ever tried to rebuild them.

Immediately after the tsunami, the government had built tin shelters which were promptly rejected by the locals. Now they have small homes made of wood and bamboo on cement stilts, which are a poor copy of traditional eco-friendly huts.

I also visited the beautiful Japanese Well, now restored to its past glory. Peering into the depths through the crystal clear water, I noticed some debris still lying at the bottom—another stark reminder of the past.

The base today is back on its feet. The happy faces of the men and women living and working there, the sound of roaring aircraft engines, the music in the evening are welcome reminders of what we had achieved in raising the station from the dust.

A tsunami warning system is in place today. Warnings are received about any seismic activity and transmitted to all stakeholders via SMS on mobile phones and through local FM stations and other means of communication.

While it is important to have a warning system in place, is it worth the amount of money it costs? We discussed this during my visit. Warnings about an impending hurricane had been received six days before Hurricane Katrina struck, and yet it was the worst natural disaster in the history of the United States.

Sophisticated instruments make it possible to predict weather patterns, but we still don't have fool-proof technology to forecast when and where an earthquake will occur. We all agreed that while warnings were necessary, it was how one acted and how information was disseminated thereafter that was most important.

We also agreed that since the community on site has to face the initial brunt of any disaster, they need to be trained and empowered to take the initial action of rescue so that fewer lives are lost. All agencies, including the Air Force, must become post-disaster managers.

Since public memory is notoriously short, it is necessary to make disaster preparedness part of a community's institutional memory. This is where our Armed Forces can help. I suggested that since we were the only military presence on the island, we could carry out community training of the locals at regular intervals. This met with general agreement.

On my last night at Car Nicobar, I was woken up in the middle of the night by thunder and lightning followed by a heavy downpour.

The bed seemed to have moved or was I imagining it?

Dismissing it as a figment of my imagination, I dozed off again. In the morning, just prior to departure, I told the Station Commander that I had imagined that the earth moved last night.

'Yes, sir,' he said. 'There was an earthquake measuring 5.7 on the Richter scale.'

The quake had lasted a few seconds and he had received an SMS from the automated tsunami warning system. Nature's gentle reminder, perhaps, that it can never be taken for granted.

Appendix

IAF Airbase Recovers from the Tsunami

Rediff.com
Archana Masih
June 24, 2005

THE INDIAN Air Force base on the Car Nicobar island was devastated in the 2004 tsunami. One hundred and sixteen IAF officers and men, their wives and children died in the disaster. Little remained of the airbase, which was established as India's southernmost defence post, a sentinel against the unseen forces lurking in regions nearby. The morning of December 26 changed all that.

In true military spirit, IAF personnel worked night and day to ensure that the airbase was operational again, just three-and-a-half months after the ocean claimed 3,513 lives in Andaman and Nicobar.

Rediff.com reports on a day in the life of the Carnic Airbase, six months after the tsunami:

When Wing Commander Sathe is through for the day in his office, he just walks around his table and arrives home.

His home is in the same room, on the left side of his large desk—across a white wooden partition that separates the office from his personal space which comprises a neat single bed, a rack of books and a handful of personal belongings. 'People can call me at any hour and I can say "I'm in office",' laughs the officer endowed with tremendous good humour.

WingCo Sathe, as he is referred to by the other officers, is the chief operating officer of the Car Nicobar Airbase. He arrived at the base—India's southernmost Air Force station in the Bay of Bengal on New Year's day, five days after the tsunami devoured the base, reducing it to a wasteland of rubble and corpses.

On April 14, the Carnic Airbase resumed operations once again. The runway is repaired, navigational aids and the basic infrastructure is in place. The operational capabilities of the station are back to normal, he says studying his presentation on a laptop, taking us through a series of 'then and now' pictures. 'In fact, we have seen more planes landing and taking off after the tsunami than before.'

In a few weeks he, and the other officers stationed there, will move out of their college kind of roomsharing arrangements in their office block to a newly-constructed living accommodation. Made of special earthquake resistant material, the quarters are very basic—one room with attached bath, two beds, separated by a table and a cupboard.

There are no frills, no luxuries and there is every possibility that officers will continue to share rooms like they have been doing these past six months. The amenities are very rudimentary but they know they are working in unusual circumstances 1,300 kms from the Indian mainland where the geographical location and the destruction of infrastructure has torn life and affected communication.

Picked up from different airbases in India, they came to Carnic immediately after the tsunami to rebuild the airbase from the dust. 'When we arrived here, all the surviving previous staff was being evacuated. They were all so distraught that we hardly had any time for the formal handing over of charge by them. We just had to pick up from scratch. We did not even know stuff like where the keys to the cupboards etc were', says Squadron Leader PM Beniwal, who had been transferred from the base in July 2004 and was reassigned to Carnic after the tsunami.

For a first-time visitor to the base, the sight can be shocking. The destruction is so overwhelming that just imagining what it must have looked like when the waters ravaged on December 26 leave you numb.

In fact, the scale of the devastation on Car Nicobar island becomes most evident only on entering the Airbase because en route all villages have been flattened, reducing them to an empty ghost land with sinister boards reading 'Erstwhile Perka, Erstwhile Small Lapathy, Erstwhile Malacca'. The 'Erstwhile' indicating where the villages and their inhabitants once stood and lived. The homes in these villages did not have much concrete and were made of wood, so they were completely washed away. 'That is why only few pillars can be seen in the debris, the rest has been flattened', says Squadron Leader Beniwal as we drive down the road on the eastern side of the island.

The Airbase, on the other end of the island, was a full-fledged helicopter station with a huge infrastructure. Around 700 staff and personnel lived there with their families. It had two schools, VIP guest houses for the air chief marshal and other visiting dignitaries, a shopping complex and homes for the station Commander, officers and air men.

The concrete rubble, the partially destroyed structures and the 160 acres of land lost to water ingress here have to be seen to understand the quantum of destruction.

Today, after six months of clearing the debris, what remains is a chilling reminder of the tragedy. Cars lie in mangled heaps, homes seem to have been blasted into unrecognisable shapes, second floors flung upside down, blackened trees lying in gigantic tangled piles. A refrigerator flung out of someone's kitchen is now lodged in the branches of a tree. 'There is a 500 per cent improvement in the quality of life now,' says the chief operating officer. 'At that time we were cutting plastic bottles into two to use them as plates and did not have spare laces for our shoes when they broke.'

The first priority was to get the runway working for relief activity and the men made use of whatever came their way—even axes to chop the wood and manually pushed it off the runway.

The 9,000 feet runway, originally measured around 3,000 feet when it was constructed by the Japanese during their occupation of the island between 1942 and 1945 in the Second World War. It was taken over by the Indian Air Force in 1956.

Forty-five tons of epoxy was used to repair the runway. The repairs began every day, post 4 pm, after the flights for the day ended. The work went on through the night till 4 am. The epoxy needed three hours to dry and the flights resumed at around 7 am.

The highest point at the airbase is on the runway, it is called Middle Marker. 'We have instructions that in the

Wildlife returns to the Island

event of an earthquake we should run towards Middle Marker,' says Sqn Ldr Beniwal standing near the erstwhile home of his friend Squadron Leader Rajshekhar who perished along with his wife and son in the tsunami.

Their daughter Meghna miraculously survived the disaster by floating on a door. She now lives with her grandmother in Hyderabad. 'I used to live across the street and used to play with Sqn Ldr Rajshekhar's children. Meghna's grandmother sent me a picture of her recently,' says Sqn Ldr Beniwal.

A few minutes later as we pass through the cluster of the wreckage of cars, Sqn Ldr Beniwal points to the remains of a gray Daewoo Matisse. 'That used to be Sqn Ldr Rajshekhar's car', he says.

The Airbase lost 116 officers, men and family to the tsunami. Those who survived were immediately evacuated, given a month's leave and subsequently transferred to other stations. The base was no longer deemed a family station and new officers and men were sent to replace, rebuild and carry out the relief operation—named Operation Madad (Help).

WingCo Sathe, who has maintained a journal of those days, remembers taking a broom and sweeping a path in a room full of glass. Since there was no water in those early days, two officers shared a 25 litre can of mineral water for bathing and ablutions.

The officers and men got down to clearing the debris, disposing the bodies and spent all their waking hours bringing some semblance of order. Rice, dal and vegetables was eaten by the officers and men from a common kitchen. Pilots who flew down as part of the relief activity sometimes stayed on to work for a month or so and would feel sad about leaving.

The first break from work came on January 16 when everyone went for a picnic.

At the peak of the relief effort, around 5,000 men were pressed into service. Around 10,000 residents were evacuated in Op Madad from the Car Nicobar island. The IAF flew around 226 sorties till January 26.

'Today there are 400 to 500 men involved on an as required basis', says Lieutenant General Aditya Singh, Commander-in-chief, Andaman and Nicobar Command.

Offices have been repaired and airmen's quarters restored. The officers dine at the temporary mess because the grand officers' mess was destroyed, and spend most of their time at work. 'Our families are not here so there is no distraction', says Sqd Leader Beniwal.

Their day begins at 5 am and work at 7 am. Lunch is around 2 pm and work officially gets over around 6 pm but there is always something to do in their 'home office'. Phone calls from HQ, visiting VIPs, liaisoning with the civil administration.

Television viewing is restricted to Doordarshan because the cable television connection is yet to be restored. At times the signal is weak and cell phones do not work, but landlines at the base are operational. Newspapers are flown in, depending on the weather. A television channel crew had to spend an extra three days on Car Nic this week because no flight could operate in the downpour. For entertainment, the staff sometimes watch a DVD/VCD, go for walks in the morning and evening and play volleyball or basketball.

Officers will serve at the base for a year-and-a-half, the

tenure for a 'hard area' posting; a regular posting lasts two to three years. The ministry of defence is looking for 170 acres away from the sea to build new housing blocks, and it is estimated it will take two years to complete the rebuilding process at the base.

'We are living normal lives now. We have come a long way from what we were to what we are today', feel the officers.

On the tarmac are a Dornier 228 and one IL 76—a huge heavy lift aircraft used to transport landmovers etc to the base. It can accommodate a helicopter in its belly. Both aircraft are ready for take off.

Tomorrow is a busy day when a delegation of MPs including the Leader of the Opposition L K Advani arrive at the base. A television crew is expected before that and a group of teachers are to arrive the following week. A chopper is to be loaded in the IL and a long queue of people walk into the aircraft.

It is after 1 in the afternoon and Wing Commander Sathe, Squadron Leader Beniwal and Wing Commander NK Atri are at the runway in the airbase they and their amazing team had come to rebuild. It is the middle of their usual day.

Carnic, Nature's Wonder

CAR NICOBAR island is truly a wonder of nature. It has been formed by the slow, painstaking process of accretion of coral larvae, live organisms that attach themselves to submerged rocks. These multiply and grow atop each other, forming a huge network of corals that finally surface above the ocean floor, forming a coral reef.

The Islands

The Nicobar Islands are believed to have been formed due to the collision of the Indo-Australian plate with the Eurasian plate. The bigger sized corals grow at the rate of about 0.3 to 2 centimetre a year, while the smaller 'branching' corals grow at the rate of about ten centimetre a year.

A rough calculation will tell you that a coral reef takes about 10,000 years to form, according to studies by the US Commerce Department's National Oceanic and Atmospheric Administration.

An island of the size of Car Nicobar would take about 20 to 30 million years to form!

Any coral island is shaped like a large mushroom with the stem holding it afloat above the water. Understandably, such islands are weak and cannot withstand earthquakes of a large magnitude.

The Coral reefs of the Car Nicobar island

The island of Car Nicobar is closer to Indonesia than it is to the Indian mainland. It is just 150 km north of Aceh in Indonesia and separated from Thailand and Burma by the Andaman Sea.

The Andaman Islands and the Nicobar Islands are actually two island groups, separated by the 10°N Parallel, with the Andaman Islands to the north of this latitude, and the Nicobar Islands to the south. To the east of the islands lies the Andaman Sea and to the west lies the Bay of Bengal.

The Nicobar group of islands has been declared a world biosphere reserve by UNESCO. All the islands south of Car Nicobar are coral islands of volcanic origin, with a huge amount of biodiversity and a very sensitive ecosystem. Of its twenty-two islands, only thirteen are inhabited. The islands are beautiful, with dense green forests and surrounded by blue-green water. The southernmost point of the islands, Indira Point, is barely 140 kilometre from Sumatra.

Car Nicobar is the district headquarters, 250 kilometre south of Port Blair. The island is shaped roughly like a rectangle, twelve kilometre by ten kilometre and is completely coral in structure.

The only defence establishment on Car Nicobar then and now is the Indian Air Force base that occupies a large area on the southern corner of the island.

Barren 1, India's only active volcano, is located on Barren Island, 135 kilometre northeast of Port Blair, the capital city. Four days after the tsunami, on December 2004, the volcano erupted because of the increased seismic activity.

... And Its Unique People

Approximately 400,000 people inhabited the islands, which occupy a land area of 6,496 square kilometre. There are a total of 572 islands in the archipelago, of which only thirty-eight are inhabited. About 40,000 people live on the Nicobar Islands, half of them on Car Nicobar. The islands have been declared a Tribal Reserve Area by an Act of Parliament. No one is permitted to visit these islands without a tribal permit issued by the administration in the capital of the islands, Port Blair.

The majority of the population here are Indians from the mainland, mostly from the eastern state of West Bengal and the southern state of Tamil Nadu.

The natives of the Andaman & Nicobar Islands are endangered groups, such as the Jarawa, Sentinelese, Shompen, Onge and Andamanese tribes, and as such, contact with most of them is restricted. They are among the world's most primitive communities and considered a link to ancient civilisations.

The natives of the Andaman and Nicobar Islands

The tribes have mostly maintained their aboriginal lifestyle for centuries, and government policy is not to interfere with them unless absolutely essential. Most of the native islanders survived the tsunami because they lived on higher ground or far from the coast. Our interaction with the local people made us realise that the tribes have inherited knowledge about tsunamis. Traditional homes in the villages are perched on stilts or machans.

The Onge (population 96, according to the 2001 census), the Jarawa (240), Sentinelese (39) and Andamanese (43) were contacted by survey teams after the tsunami and were confirmed to be safe.

The Sentinelese are isolated and live on the Sentinel Island. They are hostile to outsiders, making it difficult for officials to visit the island where they live. They have been known to shoot arrows at anyone who comes near them.

The Nicobarese, a tribe of Mongoloid descent that inhabits the Nicobar Islands, numbered 28,653 according to the 2011 census. About 700 of them perished in the tsunami and 3,000 were reported missing.

These people believe that their ancestors came from

Burma. This seems to be true when you observe their language, appearance, dress sense and habits. Nicobarese of the various islands belong to the same ethnic origin, but owing to isolation and the want of proper communication in the past, their dialects differ from island to island. They are also very good at picking up languages. English, though broken, is spoken by almost all and a large number of them have now learnt good use of Hindi too.

Nicobarese do not have any abusive words in their language. All disputes are sorted out within the community, leaving little or nothing for the local judiciary to administer.

Most of the villagers practise Christianity although I came across some Muslims too. On Sundays, one finds them at their best, clothed for the church service that all attend religiously. The women cover their heads with a veil during church service.

As beautiful as the locale, the people of Nicobar are very beautiful too. They are simple tribals who live simple lives with no major material wants.

The natives of the Andaman and Nicobar Islands who claim ancestors from Burma

Coconut oil extraction in the traditional way

There is no struggle for existence or any kind of rat race that we see in the modern society that we live in. They follow the principle of live and let live. Women do most of the work in these communities.

On a visit to any village you would find children playing in the courtyards, the chicken and pigs grazing around lazily and the men moving around leisurely.

They live together in groups and each group of families is called a *tuhet*. Each *tuhet* has a leader who takes all the decisions for the group. Many *tuhet*s make a village which has a village headman called the Village Captain, a title which came into use from visiting ships during European rule. The Captain is a hereditary post, but it has happened that headmen have been removed for non-performance. He

The newly designed homes

has one assistant headman and three to four members to help him with the management of the village. Something like our Panchayat system.

Each of the Village Captains elect a Chief Captain who becomes the chief spokesman and leader of the island.

No one 'owns' any land or any business. Business is done on behalf of and for the community as a whole. Since there is no ownership, there is no 'power' in terms of monetary values and therefore, no struggle for 'more'.

The people of Carnic in particular have now come into contact with the outside world much more as compared to the other islands and therefore the society here has changed at a faster rate.

This has also led to development of Carnic as an economic and political hub of the southern group of islands. Things have changed a bit now since the locals have been exposed to money and business. Barter system has now given way to use of money for transactions.

Nature has given abundance of food in the form of pandanus, coconut, fish and comfortable weather all around the year. Coconut is their staple food. Pandanus is like a big pineapple. It has many uses. It is eaten as a fruit, dried and made into powder and cooked, and also has medicinal properties.

Meat is generally eaten on festive occasions, pork being

the preferred meat. Fishing is done just to catch enough for a meal or two for the family. Rice has now become a staple diet on the islands, having been introduced there sometimes in the early 1900s.

People drink toddy tapped from the coconut tree.

Coconut and its byproducts are exported in huge quantities to the mainland by ships owned by businessmen. There are cooperatives formed within villages which supply the products to the businessmen to see that no exploitation occurs.

A common Nicobarese house has a small hut with a thatched roof at the centre of a clearing amidst thick vegetation. There are smaller huts around this central hut, all perched 5-6 feet above the ground. The huts include their granaries too. Ventilation for the home is provided through the floor of the house and therefore, their homes stay cool even in the summers.

Women dress up in lungies and blouses while men wear shorts and vests.

The oldest lady in Carnic, Bishop Richardson's 102-year old wife

As far as marriage customs are concerned, the Nicobarese are nearer to Western ideas. The boy selects his future wife, the matter is referred to the parents and the marriage is solemnised. No fixed rule exists that a bride must come and stay at the husband's place. It all depends on the number of males in the family—if the girl's family has lesser men then the boy shifts there or vice versa.

A large number of schools—both governmental and run by NGOs—have sprung up on the islands today. One can find a large number of children from these islands pursuing higher studies in metros. Some of the boys have now joined the Armed Forces and the police.

The locals are good athletes and enjoy various games like boat racing, wrestling and pig-fighting. The 'Hoddi' boat race is organised between the villages during March and April. Each village possesses and maintains its Hoddi boats with great care and pride.

Some sportsmen excelling in football, volleyball and other games have been absorbed into national-level teams.

Volleyball and football seem to be the most popular sport. Every village invariably has a team which keeps playing matches with one another. Sports activities generally end with a feast in the host village for all.

Just how simple the people are can be gauged through a story told by the locals. Some time ago, the government wanted to construct a road to benefit the locals but it involved cutting through some coconut plantations. This was discussed with the village chiefs and the seniors and they were offered compensation too by government officials. At the end of the briefing, all the village folk kept quiet and looked at each other. Their Captain finally broke the silence and said, 'We are all in favour of the road.'

He added, 'What we can't understand is why the government should pay compensation, after all the road is for our benefit, it's going to stay on the island and therefore, there is no need for any compensation.'

Tsunami Warnings

The fact that none of the small-sized tribes lost a life was due to the fact that these tribes stayed well inland and went to sea when they wanted to live off it.

Also, some tsunami stories had been passed down generation to generation and it appeared that they were aware of the warnings of a tsunami.

During my interaction with tribal leaders, an interesting fact came to light. There is a certain kind of red coloured fish that live at the bottom of the ocean and do not get caught in the nets usually because of the depth they live in.

The locals believe that if the red fish get caught in their nets, it a sign of an impending high-intensity earthquake and a tsunami may follow.

About four to five days prior to the 2004 December earthquake, some red fish were caught in the nets by some fishermen and a warning was sounded within the local community.

Some of the tribal leaders walked up to the district administration and warned them. However, this was seen as a figment of their imagination. Had the administration heeded to this warning—wonder if things would have been different?

Various kinds of aircraft that operated from Car Nicobar Air Base

History of the Airbase

THE JAPANESE occupied the islands in 1942, soon after the beginning of the Second World War. Until then, the British government used these islands to keep political prisoners of Indian and African origin. The Cellular Jail at Port Blair bears testimony to this fact.

Japanese Occupation
The British, during their occupation, were only interested in the Andaman group of islands which were larger and closer to mainland India. The other islands were considered strategically too small and insignificant by them.

The Japanese didn't think so and in 1942, they sent a large naval force comprising many ships, including carriers to take over the Nicobar islands. It is said that the Japanese left an indelible mark on the psyche of the population of these islands. A large number of books describe the atrocities committed during this period.

They constructed runways at Car Nicobar and Kamorta Islands. The metalled road along the perimeter of Car Nicobar to connect all the villages was constructed by the Japanese. They made use of able-bodied Nicobarese men to construct air-raid shelters, bunkers, jetties and an airfield at Car Nicobar.

The Japanese Well of the IAF Station for provision of potable water was constructed by them. The Allied Forces aircraft kept bombing the ammunition depots and Japanese warships with troops during the period.

The Japanese suspected the Nicobarese of spying for the British and 105 Nicobarese were killed by the Japanese during their occupation. Ninety of them were killed in Car Nicobar alone. They also razed the Malacca mosque to the ground, suspecting radio sets hidden underneath it.

As the logistical sustainability became more and more difficult, the Japanese began a slow withdrawal of their troops; and in 1945, the British regained control over the islands when the troops of the 116th Infantry Brigade landed here and the remaining Japanese garrison surrendered.

The Japanese finally left Carnic on 22 October 1945.

A number of Japanese officers, who had tortured the innocent Nicobarese, were punished following the Singapore trials which were held at the end of World War II.

Prior to their departure, the British were interested in resettling the Anglo-Indians and the Anglo-Burmese on these islands to form their own nation, but this never materialised.

Post-Independence, the control of the islands passed on to the Indian Union in 1950 and Andaman & Nicobar were declared a Union Territory in 1956.

Indian Military Base

In the aftermath of the Japanese surrender after World War II and the recapture of Rangoon in May 1945, the strategic importance of these islands became apparent.

Accordingly, it was decided to establish a military presence in the Andaman and Nicobar group of islands. Due to the personal intervention of then Prime Minister Jawaharlal Nehru, land was made available at Car Nicobar for the construction of an airfield.

The first airbase was called the 'No 1 Staging Post' and was established in 1956 with Squadron Leader PL Pandit as the Commanding Officer. It was primarily used as a 'staging base' for all aeroplanes flying across the Bay of Bengal.

A 3,000-feet long kutcha airstrip came into existence at that time.

In the olden days, the Dakotas flying from Barrackpore used to operate to this base, flying through Rangoon. Later, the An-12 and the versatile Fairchild Packet were used to transport heavy loads to and from these islands.

Subsequently, for many years, the IAF also deployed the Super Constellation aircraft for movement of men and material as a regular scheduled 'courier' flight.

With the passage of time, additional paramilitary and naval establishments came up in this area and the Air Force was called upon to provide the air support to maintain these troops.

Two 'Chetak' helicopters fitted with special equipment to undertake sea operations were positioned with the help of the An-12 aircraft to operate inter-island missions. Later, the much more reliable and larger Mi-8 helicopters were moved in and operated there till very recently.

In addition to the aircraft, a radar unit for air defence of the skies, along with the basic infrastructure of a full-fledged airbase was also located here, making it one of the most far flung bases of the Indian Air Force.

At the time of the tsunami, the base supported an approximate population of 2,000 which included the families of officers and airmen.

Barring the absence of families, today, the airbase is fully functional and available for round-the-clock operation. The strategic reach of the Air Force and the power projection of our country is enhanced manifold due to the availability of this base at this very strategic location.